D0399540

LEARNING TO BE

LAST

LEADERSHIP FOR
CONGREGATIONAL
TRANSFORMATION

E. LEBRON
FAIRBANKS

STAN
TOLER

BEACON HILL PRESS
OF KANSAS CITY

Copyright 2008
By E. LeBron Fairbanks, Stan Toler, and Beacon Hill Press of Kansas City

ISBN 978-0-8341-2353-3

Printed in the
United States of America

Cover Design: Chad A Cherry
Internal Design: Sharon Page

Unless otherwise indicated, all Scripture quotations are from the *Holy Bible, New International Version*® (NIV®). Copyright © 1973, 1978, 1984 by International Bible Society. Used by permission of Zondervan Publishing House. All rights reserved.

Permission to quote from the following additional copyrighted versions of the Bible is acknowledged with appreciation.

The *New American Standard Bible*® (NASB®), © copyright The Lockman Foundation 1960, 1962, 1963, 1968, 1971, 1972, 1973, 1975, 1977, 1995.

The *New King James Version* (NKJV). Copyright © 1979, 1980, 1982 Thomas Nelson, Inc.

The *Holy Bible, New Living Translation* (NLT), copyright © 1996. Used by permission of Tyndale House Publishers, Inc., Wheaton, IL 60189. All rights reserved.

The *New Revised Standard Version* (NRSV) of the Bible, copyright 1989 by the Division of Christian Education of the National Council of the Churches of Christ in the USA. All rights reserved.

The Message (TM). Copyright © 1993, 1994, 1995, 1996, 2000, 2001, 2002. Used by permission of NavPress Publishing Group.

Quotations marked KJV are from the King James Version.

Library of Congress Cataloging-in-Publication Data

Fairbanks, E. LeBron, 1942-
  Learning to be last : leadership for congregational transformation / E. LeBron Fairbanks and Stan Toler.
      p. cm.
  Includes bibliographical references.
  ISBN 978-0-8341-2353-3 (pbk.)
  1. Christian leadership. 2. Pastoral theology. I. Toler, Stan. II. Title.

  BV652.1.F37 2008
  253—dc22

                                                                    2008001061

10 9 8 7 6 5 4 3 2 1

CONTENTS

INTRODUCTION

How do you define success in Christian leadership? Be careful how you answer. It will determine your leadership *focus*. In this book we will attempt to give you insights into the kind of Christian leadership that transforms people and organizations. Our main purpose is to help you become Christlike leaders—servant leaders—who influence others to become Christlike in their mission and ministry. Our model is found in the words of the Master: "For who is greater, the one who is at the table or the one who serves? Is it not the one who is at the table? But I am among you as one who serves" (Luke 22:27). If that was His mission, then surely it should be ours!

So what is the character of this servant leadership? At its core are three compelling convictions:

- A *vision* for who we are as the people of God
- A *passion* for the work of God
- An *obsession* for how we live together as the family of God

And these convictions form the foundation of our study of effective contemporary leadership.

Conviction No. 1: Christlike Leadership Is Rooted in a *Vision for Ministry*

A vision is a consuming, fervent, and compelling inner picture. It is seeing what others do not see. At the very heart of servant leadership is a *theological vision* of our identity within the Christian fellowship. Notice the biblical imagery that defines our relationship with other Christians. We are

- "Brothers and sisters in Christ" (Col. 1:2, NLT)
- "Members together of [Christ's] body" (Eph. 3:6)
- "A fellowship of God's people" (see Acts 2:42)
- "A microcosm of the kingdom of God on earth" (see Rev. 1:6, 9)
- "A community of faith" (see Gal. 6:10)

- "A sacramental community in and through which the grace of God flows" (see 2 Cor. 9:8)

Effective Christlike leadership is grounded in these biblical perceptions of the Christian community and not just in organizational skills, although skills are needed. However, sharp skills without Christian motives easily lead to manipulation. We will discover that the primary orientation and motivation of our actions as servant leaders must be deeply theological. How much you remain captive to this conviction is directly proportional to how "successful" your leadership is judged biblically.

Affirming those with whom you work is fulfilling. But the servant leader gets equally excited about helping others succeed—regardless of where they are on their spiritual journey.

Ministry, as you know, is service to others in Jesus' name, the extension of the service of Jesus in our world. The people of God are Spirit empowered to incarnate *His* healing, guiding, sustaining, and reconciling work in the lives of those with whom they work and live. You are a *leader*. You are a *Christian*. And so you are called to this ministry of Christian leadership.

You may be called and gifted to be a pastor, teacher, evangelist, musician, or missionary, but you are on a leadership journey to use those gifts and graces to develop the gifts of others. In A *Wesleyan-Holiness Theology* the late Dr. J. Kenneth Grider reflects on his own need to grow in *grace* through *service*. In his book he gives us this prayer:

Father, I am Your bread. Break me up and pass me around to the poor and needy of this world.

I am Your towel. Dampen me with tears and with me wash the feet of people who are weary with walking and with working.

I am Your light. Take me out to where the darkness is thick, there to shine and let Christ shine.

I am Your pen. Write with me whatever word You wish, and placard the word where the least and the lost of the world will see it and read it and be helped by it.

I am Your salt. Sprinkle me on all the things that You want for people, so that my faith and love and hope will flavor their experiences.

I am Your water. Pour me into people who thirst for You but do not even know that it is You for whom they thirst. Pour into them the trust that You have helped me to place in You. Pour into them the inward witness that is in me. Pour into them the promise that soon the summer drought will pass and refreshing rivers of water will gush down over them.

I am Yours, Lord God. Use me up in what You will, when You will, where You will, for whom You will, even if it means that I am given responsibilities that are considerable and costly.[1]

Matthew 25:31-40 says that Jesus defines success in ministry as service or self-giving to others in the name—and in the place—of God. You are His instruments of instruction and care. This call and command to serve must increasingly define and shape your *vision for ministry.*

Conviction No. 2: Christlike Leadership Is Rooted in a *Passion for Formation*

Christian leadership is humble service to others in the community of faith, whose Head is Christ, for the purpose of *enabling them*—through visioning, collaboration, and example—to live their lives under His Lordship and to understand, accept, and fulfill their ministry to each other, their vocational calling, and their mission in the world.

Leadership, according to the late Dr. Harold Reed, "is known by the personalities it enriches, not by those it dominates or captivates." So, leadership within the community of faith focuses on the *qualitative growth* of the led as ministers of Jesus Christ.

This perspective on leadership raises some probing questions:

- How can *your* ministry of servant leadership enable *others* to fulfill *their* ministry to each other and *their* mission in the world?
- Are the people being served growing as Christians?
- Are they themselves becoming servants?

These are crucial concerns for leadership in the community of faith.

All Christians—even those who sometimes make life difficult—are called and gifted for the ministry of Christ. Tempting as it may be, Christian leaders will not ignore even the most "challenging" people. They will remain your responsibility—demanding keen insight, deep caring, and Spirit-empowered understanding. Are you up to the challenge?

Conviction No. 3: Christlike Leadership Is Rooted in an *Obsession for Community*

In Luke 6:40 Jesus says, "A student . . . who is fully trained will be like his teacher." Ministry is always incarnated, is always lived out in mission and ministry to others! What do you want your community—parishioners—to catch? It should be a servant spirit, committed to motivating, equipping, and enabling others to also serve in Jesus' name.

Learning to communicate a lifestyle within the community that is distinctly Christian—and self-giving at the core—is a daunting challenge. You will see that communicating right living; teaching commitments, priorities, values, and spiritual disciplines; and informing a lifestyle depends on how well *you've* lived that lifestyle.

The principle of imitation is both demanded and demanding. Herbert Mayer, in his book *Pastoral Care: Its Roots and Renewal*, reminds us that this principle was important in Christian leadership for 18 centuries. It is the Christian leader's responsibility to recapture it. Paul humbly instructed church leaders under his care to imitate him as he imitated Christ. This book will encourage you to do the same for those under your care.

The principle of imitation is the only way to effectively transfer vision, passion, and obsession within the Christian fellowship. It must possess our thinking. Ephesians 4 begins with the challenge to walk worthy of our calling as Christians and then describes what a person who walks worthy should be like. We are instructed to be gentle, humble, patient, and supportive of each other. In so living, we will "maintain the unity of the Spirit in the bond of peace" (v. 3, NRSV).

Together we will discover that Christian leaders express *gentleness*, *humbleness*, *patience*, and *supportiveness* by exercising the key leadership principle found in verse 15: "Speaking the truth in love." Christian attitudes underlie our actions and activities within the community. We are colaborers in the Body of Christ (v. 25). The people with whom we work are

God's own creation. Because of this fundamental Christian conviction, we can *be honest* with the believers; *immediate* in dealing with conflict; *up-building* with our words; and *forgiving,* even when others do not forgive us. Words and deeds done by others to us must never be permitted to create bitterness and resentment within us.

A community compulsion is a must for the servant leader; imperative, even in the throes of conflict. Because relationships are so important, we care enough to confront others with a spirit like Christ's. Caring too much about the relationship to ignore destructive behavior, we speak the truth in love. It also means allowing others to speak truthfully to us.

Again, we will see that Paul's instructions are not psychological. They are deeply theological. They are the foundations for servant leaders who are serious about leading *Christianly.* You may wonder, "What does it mean to be a servant to those I must direct in the role of authority?" or rather, "What does it mean to be a servant *in the midst* of leadership expectations and functions?"

Is servant leadership risky? You bet. Will there be misunderstandings, abuses, betrayals, or pain? Absolutely! Is it worth it? The answer is, you really don't have any choice! If you are to follow the leadership model of Christ, you must accept the risks—and serve people with humility, gentleness, patience, and encouragement.

You will be challenged. People will not see you as a finished product. Rather, they will discover that you are in the center of an ongoing process of transformation into Christlikeness (see 2 Cor. 3:18).

As you will see, your challenge is to lead from a reconciled and transformed heart. Captured by a vision for ministry, motivated by a passion for ministry formation, and characterized by an obsession for a Christlike leadership lifestyle within the community, your organization—regardless of its size—will be life giving, growth producing, and *distinctly Christian.* Increasingly, this will *empower* your people to reach out and serve others in Jesus' name.

That is Christlike leadership! To *that* ministry you are uniquely called. And you will measure your success in ministry by *that* standard!

PASSION . . .

1
SERVANT LEADERSHIP AND MINISTRY DEVELOPMENT

*The **passion** of servant leadership is grounded in a theology of ministry.*

Let's take a closer look at this.

Think of it as responding, working, and behaving like Jesus—incarnating His healing, guiding, sustaining, and reconciling work in the lives of others.

But what does this mean to the go-to person? How does this fit when the organizational pack you run in is full of bottom-line, results-driven, deadline-drawing carnivores? Does Jesus fit into this world? The natural question that arises is, "How does our relationship with Christ convert or transform our leadership lifestyle?" Or rather, how is *servant leadership* expressed in a community of faith? And what does it look like in those who reside in a community of faith but work *outside* it?

Servant Leadership and the Spiritual Life

Christian leadership begins with the leader's spiritual relationship with Christ. It is impossible for a person to be a *Christian* leader unless Christ genuinely exercises dominance in his or her heart. There are many organizations and institutions that a person can join, but the Spirit of Christ doesn't reside in them. Christianity is not a "sign on the dotted line, pay your dues, attaboy" club. The Christian faith is a deeply personal and spiritually intimate *relationship* with the God who inhabits His children. Spiritual persons are those who increasingly open themselves to the actions of God's Holy Spirit. As Christ takes control of you, your leadership style and techniques will instinctively reflect *Him*.

This means you will begin to ask new questions—questions altogether different in scope and intent than those you may have been trained to ask. You will first wonder, "How and where can I make the greatest impact for the Kingdom?" This will lead to a second question: "What changes do I need to make inwardly and in my relationship with others so that I can become a more faithful witness for Christ?" If you truly desire to be a *Christian* leader, you must first assimilate what it means to be a leader who *is* a *Christian*. Christlikeness presupposes spiritual maturity and development. Living the spiritual life means

- Identifying the presence of the Holy Spirit
- Listening with care to the Spirit's guidance
- Responding to what the Spirit says

The aim of Christian spirituality is to foster a life of holiness. "Holiness" is a word that terrifies some. It conjures up images of judgmental, religious bondage. The reality is far different. True, *scriptural* holiness is freedom. Paul explains in Rom. 6 that it is freedom from a self-serving nature bent on possessions, power, lust, and self-preservation. Holiness can never be manufactured from your good intentions. It is always delivered from above. You must begin by recognizing that such a gift is ultimately only God's to give. But it is a gift. And He insists that you take it! Foreshadowed in Leviticus, it is echoed twice under the new covenant (Eph. 1:4 and 1 Pet. 1:15-16).

Don't kid yourself. If a "positional" holiness were sufficient, the Cross would mark the end of the canon. But it doesn't. In John's Gospel, Jesus explains that His going away is a good thing, because it means that the "helper" will come. In Acts 2, we see that the Spirit is the gift that was promised. Why? Why would such a gift be necessary if God's people are hidden behind the righteousness of Christ? The New Testament writers, under inspiration, remind us that a holy God expects us to be holy. In the same way that Jesus commanded the man with the withered hand to stretch it out, our Lord is doing *in you* and *through you* what is impossible for you to do alone. Both Peter's and Paul's Epistles throw down the gauntlet: *You* be obedient . . . *you* be blameless . . . *you* be *holy*. It is God's will that you receive this gift of heart-purifying, Christ-modeling empowerment.

In the book *The Upward Call: Spiritual Formation and the Holy Life*, Drs. Morris Weigelt, Dee Freeborn, and Janine Tartaglia identified spiritual formation as "the whole person in relationship with God, within the community of believers, growing in Christlikeness, reflected in a Spirit-directed, disciplined lifestyle, and demonstrated in redemptive action in our world."[1]

Again and again, God, through His sacred Word, pleads with us to embrace a "holy consciousness":

Matt. 6:33: "But seek first his kingdom and his righteousness, and all these things will be given to you as well."

1 Cor. 2:13: "[We teach] spiritual [things] . . . spiritual[ly]."

1 Cor. 2:16: "But we have the mind of Christ."

2 Cor. 5:16: "So from now on we regard no one from a worldly point of view."

2 Cor. 4:7: "But we have this treasure in jars of clay to show that this all-surpassing power is from God and not from us."

The leader's focus must be on God. It is the first step to successful internal personal change and to outward relational impact. All that to say, you cannot, with any enduring success, be trained to do the things a Christian leader will do. You must become a Christlike individual who *leads in a Christian manner.*

With all of this in view, your understanding of what God anticipates from your relationship with Him may need a spiritual tweaking. And your *passion* for Christ may need to be recharged!

Servant Leadership and Ministry

If you are a Christian, *you are called to Christian ministry*.

In its briefest and most general understanding, ministry is *diakonia*, or service. At its very best, then, ministry (including servant leadership) is passionate service to others in Jesus' name. Certain words help us understand the dimensions of Christian ministry—words like "caring," "sharing," "growing," "relating," "teaching," and even "confronting."

Ministry—New Testament style—comes alive as someone holds the hand of a person engulfed in fear, listens intently to a person in trouble, cries with a person who is hurt, or embraces the individual who is grieving. Those broad strokes paint the picture. And that moves ministry from an ancient church in an ancient land into your hometown. Now let's park it in your driveway. Why not take an isolated, mobility-challenged senior to the store for groceries? Or why not reach deep down and find the courage to confront—in love—someone's lack of discipline or careless habits?

Serving encompasses the sharing of the Christian faith—sharing the gospel message by example or by personal witnessing, and by ministering God's Word to someone in time of need. There are two distinct temptations for the Christian who is in leadership. The first is to hide his or her faith—to compartmentalize it—as if it has no place in the marketplace. The second is to feel a deep sense of guilt if he or she cannot seem to bring those under his or her influence to a place of spiritual decision.

Brian McLaren, in his book *A New Kind of Christian*, suggests we break the chains of bondage that bind us to a bottom-line philosophy of conversions. In the emergent church movement there is a principle at work that fits very nicely into the framework of our discussion. It is not an abandonment of the Christian witness, simply a shift in expectation. McLaren encourages us to stop talking in terms of "conversions" and start logging "conversations." Sharing the gospel is less complicated than many leaders realize. Accept the fact that you do have a sphere of influence. Within that sphere, *serving* is defined by the word *relational*. When you are able to stop thinking in terms of conversions, then the chains fall away. You are free to share the gospel—specifically *your gospel*.

This is your story of what God is doing in your heart and life and relationships. This isn't Matthew's or Luke's story of Jesus. This is *your story* of how and when Christ interrupted your life and intercepted your heart. As you work to develop relationships, those who work with you will cease to be your "constituents" and will become persons—precious, sacred, God-loved souls. Your passion for their wholeness will be nothing short of Christ's. His earthly ministry embodied all of this and more, with a passion beyond our understanding.

Ministry understood in this broader sense is the setting for our specific ministry. We may be specifically called and gifted for pastoral ministry, teaching ministry, evangelism ministry, music ministry, or leadership ministry. But it is futile and self-defeating to seek to function within our specific calling while ignoring the broader calling to serve others in Jesus' name.

Jesus Defined Success in Christian Ministry as Service or Self-Giving to Others

Jesus called them together and said, "You know that the rulers of the Gentiles lord it over them, and their high officials exercise authority over them. Not so with you. Instead, whoever wants to become great among you must be your servant, and whoever wants to be first must be your slave—just as the Son of Man did not come to be served, but to serve, and to give his life as a ransom for many" *(Matt. 20:25-28).*

Your responsibility as a leader is to passionately care for God's people, as a shepherd does for his sheep, coaxing, caring, coaching, guiding, and teaching. Your leadership mandate, then, is to motivate, equip, and enable the people of God to develop their gifts and to give their lives in meaningful service to others. *Your* ministry is to prepare others for *their* ministry.

Being Christlike in Our Passionate Service, or Christian Ministry, Is a Constant in Major Theological Writings

Dietrich Bonhoeffer, in *Life Together: The Classic Exploration of Faith in Community,*[2] lists seven expressions of ministry by which a Christian community must be judged and characterized.

1. THE MINISTRY OF HOLDING ONE'S TONGUE

Here Bonhoeffer paraphrases James 3:2, "He who holds his tongue in check controls both mind and body," and references the admonishment from Eph. 4:29: "Do not let any unwholesome talk come out of your mouths." This expresses what we've been talking about. Through God's Word we are challenged to improve. Then we call on the Holy Spirit to enable those radical changes within us. Most leaders, by definition, have trouble "holding their tongue."

Leaders usually direct very *directly*. Curt, sharp, demeaning, condescending, sarcastic, caustic—these words often characterize the language and tone of leaders under the gun. But when this passage becomes absorbed by your consciousness, and the Holy Spirit changes you, then God's Word *characterizes* you. Constantly criticizing your superiors, peers, and constituents—or other unproductive, spiritually unhealthy habits, such as judging, condemning, or putting others in their place—is replaced by wholesome, healthy language that is embellished by mercy and dripping with grace.

2. THE MINISTRY OF MEEKNESS

We care more for others than for ourselves. "Do not think of yourself more highly than you ought," Paul tells us in Rom. 12:3. John tells us to make no effort to obtain the praise that comes only from God. He who serves must learn to think of others first.

3. THE MINISTRY OF LISTENING

Listening is a high-interest debt that you owe others! No wonder so many file bankruptcy under this spiritual service of leadership. A pastor who seemed to have a nearly supernatural magnetism was asked what he considered to be the secret to his ever-increasing worship attendance and outstanding percentage for staff retention. His answer: "One day a week, I do most of the talking. The other six, I make it a habit to listen."

4. THE MINISTRY OF ACTIVE HELPFULNESS

James makes it very clear. Faith without good works is a faith with dead batteries. A thriving, personal faith is active and at work in the lives of others. This is a matter of simply assisting others within the Christian community in external matters, big and small.

5. The Ministry of Bearing (Supporting)

"Carry each other's burdens" is the challenge of Gal. 6:2. "Bearing" means forbearing and sustaining one another in love. Ephesians 4:2 commands us to "be . . . humble and gentle; be patient, bearing with one another in love."

6. The Ministry of Proclaiming

This is the ministry of the Word of God. Bonhoeffer does not mean the message of Scripture proclaimed in a formal setting, such as in the worship service. He is referring to the free communication of the Word of God from person to person—to that unique situation in which one person becomes a witness in human words to another, with Christian compassion and consolation.

7. The Ministry of Authority (Leadership)

Jesus states in Mark 10:43-44, "Whoever wants to become great among you must be your servant, and whoever wants to be first must be slave of all." This is the paradox of ministry. Jesus made authority in the fellowship dependent upon brotherly service.

For Bonhoeffer, these practical expressions of Christian ministry provide the setting in which our specific ministries must function. This is particularly true as it relates to the ministry of leadership.

A study of the ministry of Christ reveals three salient features:

- *Christ the Servant.* His ministry was a servant ministry (see Matt. 20:25-28). He demonstrated His service to His Father by doing His will and to the people by accepting them as they were and meeting their needs—healing the sick, feeding the hungry, or simply taking time to be with them. Among the people, He listened to the sinner, the outcast, or the disrespectable member of society.

- *Christ the Teacher.* His ministry was mainly teaching. He taught with authority. He was known as Rabbi, "Teacher." The proclamation of the gospel, the announcement of the Kingdom to all who had ears to hear, was given in word *and* deed. It was clear teaching, adapted to the needs of the listeners and delivered in easy-to-understand illustrations and examples.

- *Christ the Sacrifice.* He was the "Lamb of God, who [took] away the sin of the world" by His sacrifice on the Cross (John 1:29). By His own free will, and in obedience to His Father, He laid down His life. His ministry was essentially sacrificial and priestly.

If we are called to be extensions of Christ, then our ministry will be characterized by *service, teaching,* and *sacrifice* to the people with whom we come in contact. It will include—to echo the words of the introduction—humble service to the community of faith, whose Head is Christ, for the purpose of enabling them, through modeling and teaching, to live their lives under the Lordship of Christ and to fulfill their ministry to each other and their mission in the world.

Servant Leadership for a Servant Community

Servant leadership mobilizes other Christians for ministry. The Christian leader models a radical commitment to building a servant community. Remember that biblically your leadership "success" will be judged in proportion to your passion toward this commitment. Will your leadership enable *others* to fulfill *their* ministry to each other and *their* mission in the world? As you consider this, ask yourself these two crucial questions:

Are the people you lead growing as Christians?

Are the people you lead becoming servants?

Robert Greenleaf, in his outstanding book *Servant Leadership*, suggests that those who are leaders must serve those whom they lead. Only those who serve, he believes, are fit for leadership. Though written for a secular audience, the book contains many thoughts on servant leadership similar to the words of Jesus.

The late Dr. Harold Reed, former president of Olivet Nazarene University and the Reed Institute for the Advanced Study of Leadership, reminds us in his book *The Dynamics of Leadership* that the quality of our leadership is largely based on our philosophy of life. If it includes a biblical theology of church and ministry, then *how* we lead—our style of leadership—will focus on the *qualitative growth* of the led as ministers of Jesus Christ, answering the call to serve others in His name.

Understood in this way, Christian ministry is a *shared ministry*, with every believer serving and supporting one another, using Holy Spirit-given gifts to stimulate personal and corporate growth and reconciliation in both the Church and the world. Ministry is a function and expression of the whole Church. It is not something that only a few persons are called, trained, and ordained to do. Rather, it is a basic function of the people of God.

Perhaps the model of ministry on the following page will help summarize this discussion and conceptualize the relationship of the leader's ministry to the ministry of the people of God whom he or she serves.

Following the diagram (fig. 1.1) full circle—from grace through the *leader* interacting with the *led*, through change among the led, and finally through producing results by the led—it becomes clear that our ministry of leadership is to prepare others for their ministries. Do you notice how the led then begin to become integrated into ministry?

Servant Leadership Vision

Vision has to do with seeing things clearly and at a great distance. In organizational and institutional thinking, it is seeing what others do not see. Vision, for the person who has it, is a consuming, passionate, and compelling inner picture. All Christian leaders are expected to have a vision for ministry. But effective Christian leaders have a shared vision. The *leader* shares the ministry vision with the *led*. Fundamental for the Christian leader is not so much *organizational vision* but rather *theological vision*.

What do we see—through the eyes of the Father—in the people with whom we work? Do we see problems or possibilities? The present or the potential? Some leaders focus only on the past. Our challenge is to see be-

Fig. 1.1

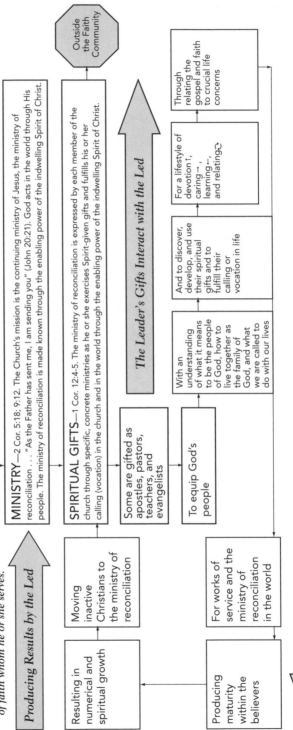

GRACE—Eph. 2:5, 8-9. We were dead. By grace through faith . . . now we are alive! God first loved the world. God initiates all activity for reconciliation and enables His children through grace to participate with Him in His ministry.

CHURCH—Eph. 2:19-22. By grace we are incorporated into God's family and become: The People of God, The Body of Christ, and The Fellowship of the Spirit.

MINISTRY—2 Cor. 5:18; 9:12. The Church's mission is the continuing ministry of Jesus, the ministry of reconciliation. . . . "As the Father has sent me, I am sending you" (John 20:21). God acts in the world through His people. The ministry of reconciliation is made known through the enabling power of the indwelling Spirit of Christ.

SPIRITUAL GIFTS—1 Cor. 12:4-5. The ministry of reconciliation is expressed by each member of the church through specific, concrete ministries as he or she exercises Spirit-given gifts and fulfills his or her calling (vocation) in the church and in the world through the enabling power of the indwelling Spirit of Christ.

Outside the Faith Community

The Leader's Gifts Interact with the Led

Change Among the Led

The relationship between the ministry of the pastor/teacher and the ministry of the community of faith whom he or she serves.

Producing Results by the Led

Some are gifted as apostles, pastors, teachers, and evangelists

To equip God's people

With an understanding of what it means to be the people of God, how to live together as the family of God, and what we are called to do with our lives

And to discover, develop, and use their spiritual gifts and to fulfill their calling or vocation in life

For a lifestyle of devotion↑, caring→, learning←, and relating↻

Through relating the gospel and faith to crucial life concerns

Moving inactive Christians to the ministry of reconciliation

Resulting in numerical and spiritual growth

For works of service and the ministry of reconciliation in the world

Producing maturity within the believers

yond the past, or even the present with its up-front problems—to see redeemed individuals who are called to live as an extension of Jesus in their world, incarnating His healing, sustaining, and reconciling work in the lives of others.

Again as leaders, we must have a consuming, passionate, compelling inner picture of

- *Who* we are as the people of God
- *How* we may live together as the family of God
- *What* we are called to do with our lives in the work of God

And servant leadership is the *transference* of this vision. We must transfer our vision of ministry to those for whom we have Christian care and responsibility; they will in turn transfer their vision to others! More and more we need to see ourselves as *equippers* of ministers. Unfortunately, most of us have been educated to be ministers, not to be *enablers* of ministers.

Shared ministry demands "deep seeing" and "deep visioning." Only the person who can see the *invisible* can do the *impossible*. Questions such as "What if?" or "Why not?" ought to permeate our Christian leadership mind-set.

Elton Trueblood states it most clearly:

> Unless the layman is given solid teaching, his ministry, after an initial burst of freshness, will tend to degenerate into little more than a string of trite phrases linked to commonplace ideas and buttressed by a few sloppily quoted biblical passages. We must take the education of the laity with utter seriousness. Lay persons are not assistants to the pastor, to help him do his work. Rather, the pastor is to be their assistant; he is to help equip them for the ministry to which God has called them. The difference is as revolutionary as it is total. Half measures are worse than nothing. Our hope lies in making big plans, in undertaking to produce a radical change, in aiming high. Adult education is the big thing in the church. It is not a decoration, it is the centerpiece.[3]

Only from this perspective will ministry be mutually understood and shared. And without this shared vision, vibrant ministry in and through a

Christian organization, is as probable as a two-sided triangle. Ministry happens when the *leader* and the *led* have a common vision and pursue it together. The more consuming the vision, the greater the commitment to ministry.

You must be captured by a vision that transcends ministry to the people and for the people, to ministry with the people and by the people. Our leadership ministry is in helping others understand and develop *their* ministry.

PASSION . . .

2

DEVELOPING A STRATEGY FOR SERVANT LEADERSHIP

So how do you communicate a vision of ministry so that others will come to share it? Jesus challenges us in Luke 6:40: "A student who is fully trained will be like his teacher." True ministry leadership is always incarnated—fleshed out in the lives of others. Paul encouraged, "Follow my example, as I follow the example of Christ" (1 Cor. 11:1).

But what is it about ourselves that we want future leaders to flesh out in their own lives? There are several characteristics:

A Servant Spirit That Is Committed to Motivating, Equipping, and Enabling Others

You must communicate your passion and vision to see others enter the ministry cycle. This is success for the Christian leader. And this is what it means to be a servant leader.

A Lifestyle That Is Distinctly Christian and Self-Giving

How do you teach commitments, priorities, values, and spiritual disciplines? How do you teach a lifestyle? For Paul, it was through personal example. In teaching his disciples how to be set apart from the attitudes of the world, he said, "For you yourselves know how you ought to follow our example. We were not idle when we were with you, nor did we eat anyone's food without paying for it. On the contrary, we worked night and day, laboring and toiling so that we would not be a burden to any of you. We did this, not because we do not have the right to such help, but in order to make ourselves a model for you to follow" (2 Thess. 3:7-9).

Others must see servant leadership qualities in you if you are to effectively transfer your vision of ministry to them.

A Walk Worthy of Our Calling

The traits found in Eph. 4 follow the challenge: Be gentle, humble, patient, and supportive of each other. In so living, we will "maintain the unity of the Spirit in the bond of peace" (v. 3, NRSV).

But as Christian leaders, how do you express gentleness, humbleness, patience, and supportiveness? The key is found in verse 15: "Speaking the truth in love." The concept is fleshed out in verses 25-32:

- Because as Christians *we are God's family*, we should speak truthfully and not lie to one another (v. 25).
- Because when we do not speak the truth in love, *Satan gets a foothold in our lives*. We should not postpone dealing with our anger and should deal with our differences in a Christian way (vv. 26-27).
- Because of the *power of words to heal and affirm*, we should be supportive and uplifting, avoiding negative talk (v. 29).
- Because *we have been forgiven in Christ*, we should be forgiving, not holding grudges and becoming resentful (vv. 31-32).

Paul is not talking about administrative techniques but Christian attitudes that support your actions and activities. You are a colaborer in the Body of Christ (see v. 25). Never lose sight of your connection to and dependence on the *whole* Body. Reprogram your thinking so that you can function with others out of an I-you frame of reference. Understand that the people with whom you work are God's own creation.

A Determination Not to Use Others as a Means to an End

Ignoring our family relationship with Christ and treating fellow members of His family as persons to be manipulated for our own purposes gives

Satan a foothold. The enemy of our soul laughs at unresolved conflict that divides the fellowship of the faithful. We must see people as fellow workers in a shared ministry.

A Use of Words as Channels of God's Grace (See Eph. 4:30)

According to Paul, dialogue is a sacrament. And God's forgiveness frees us to take the initiative in forgiving those who hurt us. When we fail to live by these guidelines as a Christian community, the Spirit of God is grieved (Eph. 4:30). Verses 25-32 reveal the means by which we "maintain the unity of the Spirit in the bond of peace" (v. 3, NRSV) and in so doing, walk (lead) worthy of our calling (see v. 1).

Again, because of these fundamental Christian attitudes, you can be honest with believers, immediate in dealing with conflict, and upbuilding in your words.

Frequently express thoughts that communicate

I love you,

I accept you,

I respect you,

I need you,

I trust you,

I serve you,

and I forgive you.

When we do this, words and deeds done *to us* will not create bitterness *within us*.

A Courage That Cares Enough to Confront

Yes—relationships with your brothers and sisters in Christ are *that* important.

When Christian leaders perceive words or deeds of others to be harmful to their growth or to the growth of the fellowship, they care enough to confront the action—in the Spirit of Christ and according to biblical principles (Matt. 18:15-17).

The basic question is always, "How can we live together as Christians so that our relationships are redemptive and a witness to unbelievers of the reconciling work of God in Christ?" The question is not only psychological but also deeply theological. The Spirit of God is concerned with the communications of His people (see Eph. 4:30).

Your assignment, then, is greater and more demanding than communicating facts or numbers. Your responsibility is to encourage a passionate, Christian-servant lifestyle that motivates, equips, and enables those whom we lead to *serve others in Jesus' name.*

If your vision of ministry and your leadership lifestyle is characterized by Eph. 4:25-32, then those whom you serve—and for whom you are responsible—will increasingly adopt it as their ministry model. But they will not see in us a finished product. Instead they will discover in us the ongoing process of our being transformed into the likeness of Christ.

A Checking of Motives

We must continually ask ourselves, "What does it mean to be a servant to those within my charge?" "What does it mean to be a servant in the midst of the expectations, roles, and functions of leadership?"

And what about the risks? What about misunderstandings? Abuses? Betrayals? Pain? Hurts? *Is it really worth the risk of being a servant leader?*

If we are to follow Christ's example, then it is absolutely worth the risk! Out of His pain—and from His risk—a whole company of committed followers were inspired to evangelize the world and to disciple believers, until they were able to launch their own ministries.

Lead with a vision to serve and with a commitment to equip servant leaders! If you are captured by this vision of ministry formation and are characterized by a servant leadership lifestyle, then your group—regardless of its size—will be life giving, growth producing, and *distinctly Christian.*

What mark will you leave behind when you depart your present leadership assignment? What sign will tell a future traveler that you have existed? The deepest impressions will be made in those moments when you say, "I am your brother or sister. I will serve you in Jesus' name, regardless of the cost."

POWER ● ● ●

3
UNDERSTANDING
THE SOURCE
OF THE
LEADER'S
POWER

*The **power** of servant leadership is rooted in a
relentless pursuit of Christlikeness.*

Dr. Robert Mulholland said, "Spiritual formation is the process of being conformed to the image of Christ for the sake of others." Using figure 2.1, below, we see that the spiritual, emotional, and organizational power involved in leading the people of God may appear to reside in us (Leadership Model B); but in fact, that power comes from Christ (Leadership Model A). This power is something that sincere Christian leaders are continually pursuing, hence the circular diagram. Your leadership style (B) is a reflection of how you respond to the power that Christ has already offered (A). Most of this chapter will explore Leadership Model B. However, at the outset, it is essential to take a moment to explore Leadership Model A.

Fig. 2.1

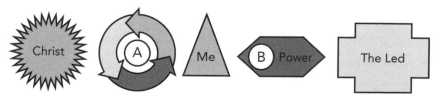

The Book of Exodus tells us that God instructed Moses to lead His people out of Egypt. When Moses hesitated and asked God to send someone else, God underscored the concept of leadership (Model A, fig. 2.1). Not only did God reassure Moses of His constant presence, saying He would be with him, but He also assured him of His constant *power* and support for his administration. That's seen in the "credentials" He presented to the leader:

Moses said to God, "Who am I, that I should go to Pharaoh and bring the Israelites out of Egypt?" And God said, "I will be with you. And this will be the sign to you that it is I who have sent you: When you have brought the people out of Egypt, you will worship God on this mountain." Moses said to God, "Suppose I go to the Israelites and say to them, 'The God of your fathers has sent me to you,' and they ask me, 'What is his name?' Then what shall I tell them?" God said to Moses, "I AM WHO I AM. This is what you are to say to the Israelites: 'I AM has sent me to you'" *(Exod. 3:11-14).*

In discussing Christian leadership, the late Professor Henri J. M. Nouwen confirmed that both Leadership Models A and B (fig. 2.1) are the basis of a Christian leader's authority, or power.

Leadership in the Name of Jesus

Printed in 1989, the material in Nouwen's book *In the Name of Jesus: Reflections on Christian Leadership*[1] was first presented to a group of Roman Catholic leaders in Washington, D.C., on the subject of Christian leadership in the 21st century. Several years earlier, Nouwen had moved to Daybreak, one of the L'Arche worldwide communities for mentally handicapped people. The move to Daybreak in Toronto followed a brilliant teaching career at Harvard, Yale, and Notre Dame.

The brief, yet powerful, book of 81 pages describes a vision of Christian leadership nurtured in a life of prayer, confession, and forgiveness. Nouwen addresses three contemporary temptations of Christian leaders: to be relevant, to be spectacular, and to be powerful. He was guided in his vision by two stories from the Gospels: the story of Jesus' temptation in the desert (Matt. 4:1-11) and the story of Peter's call to be a shepherd (John 21:15-19).

According to Nouwen, Christian leadership is a matter of self-denial, and it leads from a position of vulnerability to God's power (Leadership Model A in fig. 2.1). He identifies three "movements" in the book:

- From Relevance to Prayer
- From Popularity to Ministry
- From Leading to Being Led[2]

Relevance

Certainly the leader should not be *unaware* of what is happening in the world; but he or she should not be *absorbed* by it. Jesus taught that in His prayer for His disciples: "My prayer is not that you take them out of the world but that you protect them from the evil one. They are not of the world, even as I am not of it" (John 17:15-16). The phrase "even as I am not of it" is captivating. No one spoke clearer to society than the Master. His use of parables, for example, brought heavenly truths within earthly reach. But His agenda was not about fitting in with the crowd. Rather, He wanted to lead the crowd to the Kingdom.

While you may seek to make your message and method relevant to your circle of leadership, your highest aim is to be on your higher calling: an uncompromising commitment to the will and the work of God, motivated by the power of God.

Popularity

Remember the second temptation of Jesus? It was a temptation to do something spectacular—something that would bring the applause of people; something that would highlight His personal power (B in fig. 2.1). "Throw yourself from the parapet of the temple and let the angels catch you and carry you in their arms," the enemy told Jesus (see Matt. 4:5-6). The discipline needed to counter this temptation is "confession and forgiveness." Nouwen reminds us that in our own strength we cannot heal, reconcile, or give life to others. We are "wounded people," who need as much care as anyone we care for. "The mystery of ministry," Nouwen proclaims, "is that we have been chosen to make our own limited and very conditional love the gateway for the unlimited and unconditional love of God."[3]

For us as well, the discipline required to overcome the temptation of "heroism" is confession and forgiveness—personal brokenness and a willingness to ask for forgiveness from those to whom we minister.

In faith communities, leaders are "accountable to them, and need their affection and support, and are called to minister with their whole being, including their wounded selves."[4]

Power and Control

The third temptation of Jesus was the temptation of power. "I will give you all the kingdoms of this world in their splendor" (see Matt. 4:8-9), Jesus was told by Satan (Leadership Model B, fig. 2.1). Is this an irresistible temptation? Nouwen reminds us that power provides for us a substitute for "the hard task of love, control over the cross, being a leader over being led."[5] Power and control often replace, Nouwen believes, healthy, intimate relationships with the faith community.

Jesus modeled this principle in a stirring way in John 21:18. The greatest surrender of power and control is the Cross. There, the Creator victoriously conquered temptation and voluntarily surrendered to the created. He had the power to reverse the circumstances, but He surrendered it. Forever more, the led would be challenged by their leader to live a life of humble and sacrificial service.

Leading with the Mind of Christ

Nouwen challenges Christian leaders to think theologically about the practice of leadership—thinking and leading with the mind of Christ. Christian leaders of the future need "to be theologians" who "know the heart of God" and reflect His presence in the midst of the many seemingly irreconcilable expectations placed upon them in their particular ministry assignments.[6] In referring to leading with the mind of Christ, Nouwen presents a theological leadership: a deep spiritual formation involving the whole person—body, mind, and spirit.

Our challenge, according to Nouwen, is "to move from a concern for relevance," popularity, and power "to a life of prayer, . . . communal and mutual ministry," and "leadership in which we critically discern where God is leading us and our people."[7]

Questions About Leadership

To be effective leaders, we must develop the skills appropriate in our relationships with the led. We must ask ourselves the difficult questions about spiritual leadership:

- Do my gifts match the task?
- Can I do this task alone?
- Must I be the one who is always in charge?

Character must always be the overriding focus for the servant leader. Paul said,

> Your attitude should be the same as that of Christ Jesus: Who, being in very nature God, did not consider equality with God something to be grasped, but made himself nothing, taking the very nature of a servant, being made in human likeness. And being found in appearance as a man, he humbled himself and became obedient to death— even death on a cross! Therefore God exalted him to the highest place and gave him the name that is above every name, that at the name of Jesus every knee should bow, in heaven and on earth and under the earth, and every tongue confess that Jesus Christ is Lord, to the glory of God the Father *(Phil. 2:5-11)*.

We must look at our spirit, strategy, style, and stewardship as it relates to that of Christ Jesus. We must consider our likeness in regard to *His likeness*, among *His people*, from *His fullness* and for *His glory*.

A Biblical Model for Leading in a Faith Community (Eph. 4)

Virginia Satir said, "Communication is the greatest single factor affecting one's personal health and his/her relationship to others."[8] That leads again to the highly important leadership question mentioned earlier: "How can we live together, so that our relationships are redemptive and a witness to unbelievers of the reconciling work of Christ?" That is, "How does my Christian leadership enable others to fulfill their ministry to each other and their mission in the world?"

- In the midst of conflicting expectations, multiple constituents, differing denominational backgrounds, various levels of maturity, multicultural perspectives, how can we live together *Christianly?*
- How does a holiness doctrine influence a holiness lifestyle? How does our holiness testimony translate to a Christian leadership lifestyle? Going back to figure 2.1, how does "A" translate into an effective and correct "B"? As missionaries in cross-cultural situations, or pastors in local churches, these questions become critical for us.

In the setting of our ministry, we are in a close Christian community and we quickly become aware of others' strengths and weaknesses. Our own personality differences soon become obvious. Thus, our specific leadership setting becomes a dynamic laboratory for learning how to live together as God's family.

We must ask ourselves, *How do I respond to conflict under pressure? Do I respond "Christianly," or in a way that is no different from the person who makes no profession of faith?* Why are these issues so important? There are several important keys:

Key Challenge: Walking "worthy" of our calling (Eph. 4:1-3)

Ephesians 1—3 provides statements of fact. The chapters are doctrinal and explain who we are in Christ. Ephesians 4—6 challenges us with commands to action. These chapters are ethically focused and explain how we should live as Christians. Ephesians 4:1 is the transition verse that invites us to walk *worthy* of *our calling* and to participate with God in the reconciliation of the world back to himself.

Key Insight: Living (and leading) the reconciled and transformed life (Eph. 4:2-3)

If living and leading a reconciled and transformed life is our calling, then how does this happen? Ephesians 4:2-3 tells us, "Be completely humble and gentle; be patient . . . be supportive of one another in love. . . . Make every effort to keep the unity of the Spirit in the bond of peace."

Paul demonstrated reconciliation with God by living redemptively within the fellowship. When you do this, you will have credibility to tell unbelievers, "You need to be reconciled to God." If God is more interested in our character than our comfort, then what are the character qualities God wants us to demonstrate within the Christian community?

Second Peter 1:5-9 says,

> For this very reason, make every effort to add to your faith goodness; and to goodness, knowledge; and to knowledge, self-control; and to self-control, perseverance; and to perseverance, godliness; and to godliness, brotherly kindness; and to brotherly kindness, love. For if you possess these qualities in increasing measure, they will keep you from being ineffective and unproductive in your knowledge of our Lord Jesus Christ. But if anyone does not have them, he is nearsighted and blind, and has forgotten that he has been cleansed from his past sins.

If we possess these qualities, we will be productive and effective in our Christian walk. How do we develop these character qualities and walk "worthy," in humility, gentleness, patience, supportiveness, and unity?

Key Principle: "Speaking the truth in love" (Eph. 4:15)

"Speaking the truth in love" is a powerful biblical concept for leaders of Christian communities. It is an enabling principle to embrace and lead the people of God. However, the skill of "making contact" is not automatically received when we are filled with God's Spirit in the experience of entire sanctification.

Our challenge is to lead from a reconciled and transformed heart. Captured by a vision for ministry, motivated by a passion for ministry formation, and characterized by an obsession for a Christlike leadership lifestyle within the community, the faith community for which we are responsible—regardless of its size—will be life giving, growth producing, and *distinctly Christian*. Increasingly, this will *empower* our responsibility groups to reach out and serve others in Jesus' name.

In the next chapter we will discuss another important key. It's the application key. We'll discover how the source of power is communicated through Christian leadership.

POWER ● ● ●

4

THE
COMMUNICATION
OF
POWER

Principles without "hands and feet" are mere paper decorations. How does the Christian leader move from source to service—how do we communicate the *power* principles to those we lead so that they will communicate them to others? There is an another key. It is the *Key of Application:* The principle applied (Eph. 4:25-32). Figure 2.2 is a communication model for leading the people of God, titled Speak the Truth in Love.

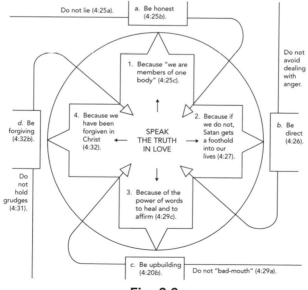

Fig. 2.2

James warned that an unruly tongue can lead to spiritual and organizational anarchy: "Likewise the tongue is a small part of the body, but it makes great boasts. Consider what a great forest is set on fire by a small spark. The tongue also is a fire, a world of evil among the parts of the body. It corrupts the whole person, sets the whole course of his life on fire, and is itself set on fire by hell" (James 3:5-6).

Conversely, the tongue under the control of the Holy Spirit is restorative. It speaks from a Christ-filled heart. By virtue of being born again into the family of God, Christian leaders are children of truth. Their leader, the Lord Jesus Christ, describes himself as being "the truth" (John 14:6). So those who follow Him not only flesh out His truth but also are called to communicate it in a loving and positive way. Paul, the apostle who called Christians to follow him as he followed Christ, encouraged his students to let the character of Christ be the motivating power factor in their communication, speaking the truth in love. Why?

We "Speak the Truth in Love" Because We Are Members of One Body (Eph. 4:25)

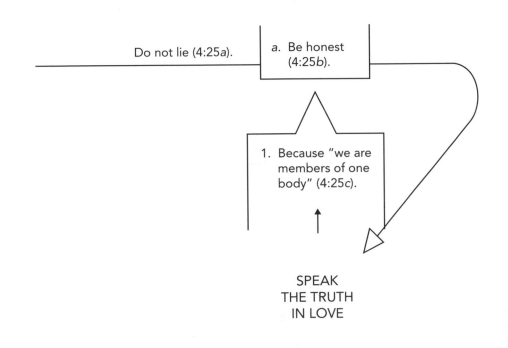

Do not lie (4:25a).

a. Be honest (4:25b).

1. Because "we are members of one body" (4:25c).

SPEAK
THE TRUTH
IN LOVE

The Bible compares the spiritual body—the Body of Christ—to the physical body (1 Cor. 12:12-27; Rom. 12:3-8; Eph. 4:1-6). What a difference it makes when we affirm—even in situations of disagreement or conflict—that the person "across the table" from us, on the basis of his or her testimony of faith, is a member with us of the Body of Christ.

In Paul's letter to the Ephesians, he has much to say to us about our conversations with others. Because of our conviction to speak the truth in love we should "put off falsehood" (Eph. 4:25), that is, we should not lie.

The verse applies to us personally in areas of emotional dishonesty, such as when we are not honest about our negative feelings toward others and yet erect barriers between them and ourselves. John Powell explains the levels of communication about which we speak:

- Lowest level—the level of cliché
- Next level—the level of facts
- A higher level—the level of ideas
- An even higher level—the level of feelings[1]

In verse 25, Paul encourages us to be honest. That implies far more than an absence of lies. It implies the kind of honesty that allows others to know us as we are, secure in our acceptance by God, and based on the affirming experience of love.

Even when under attack, the apostle opened his heart to others to share with them his inner feelings and experiences (2 Cor. 1:3-9; 2:1-4). He could claim without hesitation that those who met him came to understand his motives fully (1 Thess. 2). This trait of honesty in relationships personally and with others had a countermodel in some of the Pharisees. They were hypocritical because they were usually playacting, deceiving themselves as well as attempting to deceive others. The Pharisees were the one group that generally prevented both Jesus' truth and touch from reaching them. They had lived in their own world of pretense and were cut off from all that could have saved them.

John deals with the issue of honesty in his first Epistle. Insisting that we "walk in the light," he first asks us to be honest with ourselves—and then with others—about our sins and failings (1 John 1:5-10). Freedom to know God's cleansing comes only with honesty about our sins and a confession of them. Likewise, honesty and confession in the fellowship of believers is imperative.

Why is it so important? Remember, Paul refers to us as members of one Body. Look up the following references, which were listed earlier, and read Paul's description of our relationship to one another:

- 1 Corinthians 12:12-27
- Romans 12:3-8
- Ephesians 4:1-6

We Speak the Truth in Love Because When We Do Not, Satan Gets a Foothold in Our Lives

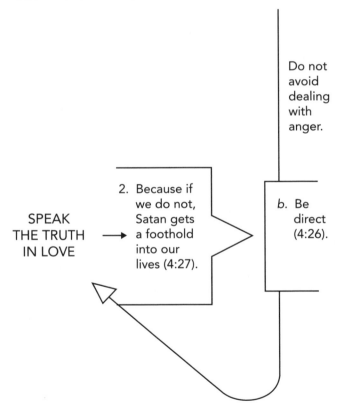

Ephesians 4:26-27 says, "'In your anger do not sin': Do not let the sun go down while you are still angry, and do not give the devil a foothold."

Dealing with unresolved anger isn't an option for the Christian leader. Until he or she learns to deal with inner conflict, the possibility of resolving conflict in the corporate community will be challenging.

Conflict Management

As long as there are human beings in your organization, there will be human conflict. It is important to consider the issue of conflict—especially within the Christian community.

The first step in managing that corporate conflict is to realize the main issue. The goal is not conflict resolution but *conflict management* in a *Christian manner*—understanding but not necessarily agreement. There is great concern about conflict. Too often we use avoidance tactics in conflict situations—instead of confronting an issue, we deny it by not talking about it.

When we use the avoidance tactic, we believe the real issue will eventually go away if we keep putting it off until tomorrow. We make the unscriptural assumption that peace-loving Christians should always get along and not have serious conflicts. We all know this isn't true, but we still avoid the issue. Why?

- We deny our real feelings, harbor resentment, and allow the bitterness to intensify.
- We lack the knowledge to deal creatively with conflict situations.
- We're afraid to share our honest feelings for fear of rejection, disapproval, frustration, or hurt.
- We want to protect our "image" of being kind, understanding, and loving.

Conflict Defined

Conflict is what develops between individuals when they differ in their opinion about plans, programs, or personnel. David Augsburger, in his book *Caring Enough to Confront,* says, "When your thrust as a person runs counter to mine, to deny my own thrust is to be untrue to the push and the pull of God within me. For me, to ignore and do violence to your thrust as a person is to violate your becoming a Son of God."

Augsburger says that "conflict is natural, normal and neutral. Conflict is neither good nor bad, right nor wrong. . . . How we view, approach and work through our differences does to a large extent determine our whole life pattern."[2] So the question is not *will* conflict arise? The question is *how will* we deal with it?

CONFLICT MANAGEMENT EXAMPLES

Virginia Satir[3] explains how we normally deal with conflict situations. Ninety-six percent of troubled families deal with conflict in one of four inappropriate ways: placating or giving in; blaming; withdrawing; and distracting.

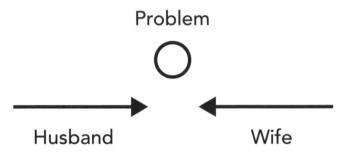

The result of using inappropriate ways to deal with conflict is that the problem remains, tension mounts, and relationships begin to crumble.

There is a fifth option: "I care enough to confront" (Augsburger), "leveling with love" (Satir), or "speak the truth in love" (Eph. 4:15). This grace-given option is the gift and freedom to share your negative and positive feelngs with the very people you need to share the emotions. It avoids the harboring of resentment and bitterness over words spoken to you or actions taken against you, your family, or your friends.

ARMS OF GENUINE RELATIONSHIP

"Care-fronting" or "leveling" as referred to by Augsburger is the biblical principle of "speaking the truth in love." This option brings healing, enables growth, and produces change, but only 4 percent of us deal with conflict in this manner. There are two arms of a genuine relationship: (1) confrontation with truth and (2) affirmation of love.

Reaching out is two-armed. The right hand reaches out: *I do care; I want to respect you; I want your respect.* And then the left: *I want you to know how I feel; I want to tell you where I am; I have this goal for our relationship.* This "caring and confronting" approach ends the blame game and gets to healing questions—in simple, clear, direct language. What is the loving, responsible, truly respectful thing to do? So how do you begin to manage conflict in a "caring and confronting" way?

STEPS IN CONFLICT MANAGEMENT

1. ELIMINATE A WIN-LOSE MENTALITY (I'm right; you're wrong). There are three aspects of the win-lose mentality: (1) I win; you lose (authoritarian); (2) you win; I lose (permissiveness); (3) no win (negativism).

2. TRY TO TRULY HEAR WHAT ANOTHER SAYS. This way of listening—known as active listening—strains to hear how something is said and what feelings are conveyed. It involves hearing with an *inner ear* to the hurts, angers, and the demands of the other person.

3. USE "I" MESSAGES INSTEAD OF "YOU" MESSAGES. "I" messages reflect my feelings without placing blame. "You" messages are most often attacks, criticisms, fault-finding—ways of fixing blame. There is a tremendous difference between an honest confession ("I" message) and distorted rejection ("You" message).

"I" message	"You" message
I am angry.	You make me angry.
I feel rejected.	You're judging and rejecting me.
I don't like the wall between us.	You're building a wall between us.
I don't like being blamed.	You're blaming everything on me.

4. ELIMINATE "WHY" QUESTIONS. "Why" questions are an effective way of manipulating others, similar to "You" messages.

"Why must I always complete the work you begin?"

"Why don't you follow through on your projects?"

"Why don't you show a little interest in others?"

"Why can't I get a little cooperation?"

"Why" questions have hidden messages of anger that we are unwilling to own honestly. "Why" questions are a hit-and-run way of dealing with others.

5. GIVE CLEAR SIGNALS. Initiate a clear discussion. "Speaking the truth in love" gives clear "yes" or "no" signals. "Yes" signals come easy. However, "no" signals are more difficult—especially face-to-face. Often we hesitate to clearly state our feelings for fear of rejection or disapproval of others. Jesus said, "Let your 'Yes' be 'Yes' and your 'No', 'No'" (Matt. 5:37).

6. ACCEPT ANGER AS A NATURAL HUMAN EMOTION. Clear statements of anger are different from feelings and demands. Clear statements are a positive emotion, a self-affirming emotion that responds to the heart of rejection and devastation. There are two types of anger to consider: (1) personal anger and (2) virtuous anger (which is anger focused on deeds not persons). Virtuous anger can slice through emotional or communication barriers and establish contacts.

7. SEEK TO BE CHRISTLIKE IN RESPONDING TO CONFLICT. "Speaking the truth in love" is the Christlike response to conflict. It evidences a Christian lifestyle that cares enough to confront, and yet seeks to be redemptive (Eph. 4:15-32). When differences between people are dealt with openly, conflict can be a positive experience because it can lead to personal growth. But when differences are concealed and individuals are prevented from expressing themselves, personal growth will not occur.

Personal conflict is a part of growing up and trying out new capabilities—learning the value of expressing differences openly and listening to the other person's response in the hope of reaching some sort of understanding.

KEY QUESTIONS FOR CONFLICT MANAGEMENT

Key questions to ask in the midst of conflict situations are, *What can I learn?* and *How can I change?* (growth-producing questions). Conversely, growth-inhibiting questions are, *Why me?* or *What if . . . ?* (a could-have, should-have, would-have way of thinking).

We Speak the Truth in Love Because of the Power of Words to Heal and to Affirm (Eph. 4:29)

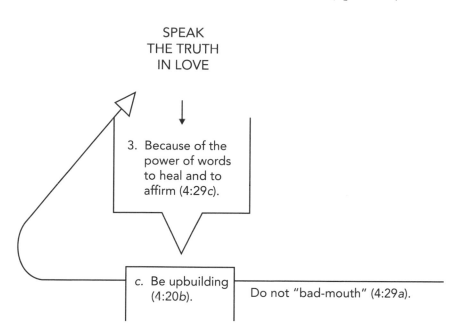

Speak "only what is helpful for building others up according to their needs" (v. 29). Paul encourages members of the Body to use their speech for the help of others, for their upbuilding as the occasion may offer.

Dialogue Is a Sacrament

Our speech is to be used for the spiritual benefit of those who are linked with us in the Body of Christ. Dialogue is a sacrament. We are to converse with each other in such a way that our words become a demonstration of the very grace of God.

For Paul, there is no room for empty chatter or for remarks that degrade another person. He says, "Do not let any [corrupt or] unwholesome talk come out of your mouths" (Eph. 4:29). Corrupt talk is foul talk. Colossians 4:6 reads, "Let your conversation be always full of grace, seasoned with salt, so that you may know how to answer everyone." In biblical anthropology, the mouth is representative of the whole body and reveals the whole man. In Matt. 12:34 Jesus says, "Out of the overflow of the heart the mouth speaks."

Speech Reveals the Quality of Our Relationship with Christ

Paul emphasized that a person's speech reveals the quality of his or her relationship with Christ. He is not talking about a technique but rather an attitude toward the other person.

- *I need you*—you have gifts and strengths I don't possess to affirm, disciple, correct, build up.
- *I love you*—you are my brother/sister in Christ.
- *I accept you*—you are being changed by Christ as I am being changed.
- *I trust you*—you desire to serve the same Christ I serve.
- *I respect you*—you are different, yet we are one in Christ.
- *I serve you*—I want to minister grace to you.

Praise-to-Criticism Ratio

In "speaking the truth in love," we must have a focus beyond ourselves, beyond self-serving comments. Our focus must be on the upbuilding of others. Be positive in your communication. Make sure you make more positive than negative statements about other people. Listen for your praise-to-criticism ratio.

Some very personal and practical questions to consider from Eph. 4:29 about the use of words are these:

- Do I tend to "bad-mouth"?
- Do I tend to shoot from the hip?
- Do I tend to respond quickly before I have all the facts?
- Do I tend to talk about people behind their backs, saying things I would not say to them?
- Do I tend to stress unimportant issues?
- Do I tend to make excuses?
- Do I tend to avoid reality questions?
- Do I tend to use unfair communication techniques? (Unfair communication techniques present problems with what we say and problems with what we don't say.)

Consider these questions about the use of our words within the community of faith:

- Does what I say build up or tear down the other person?
- Would I say what I am saying directly to the person involved?
- Do I know all the facts or am I responding on the basis of half-truths or partial facts?
- Is my response triggered more by emotion than by reason?
- Is the issue really deserving of the action and energy that I am giving it?
- Can the situation be seen from a different perspective?
- Have I tried to accept the feelings of the other person and understand why the person feels the way he or she does?

In dealing with others, remember, the person beside you is different only until you get to know him or her. If it doesn't make a difference, don't let it make a difference.

The Power to Bless

Ephesians 4:28 tells us to steal no longer. Exodus 20:16 says, "You shall not bear false witness against your neighbor" (NKJV). The broader implications prohibit the sin of slander, tale-bearing, gossip, flattery, and character assassination. To destroy a man's character by a whispering campaign profits nothing. As Shakespeare put it, "Who steals my purse steals trash; . . . But he that filches from me my good name; Robs me of that which not enriches him, and makes me poor indeed" (*Othello*, Act III, Scene 3, Line 183).

Christian leaders have the power to bless and to withhold blessings—to cause others to grow or to wither, to help or to hinder, to heal or to hurt. The person who can speak the sincere word of forgiveness and acceptance is a healer of the highest order. Why? Because he or she removes the deep malady of the inner curse and condemnation. Paul is concerned with the role of words exchanged between individuals within the Body. In the midst of everyday dialogue, God's grace and power should flow through words used.

We Speak the Truth in Love Because We Have Been Forgiven in Christ (Eph. 4:31-32)

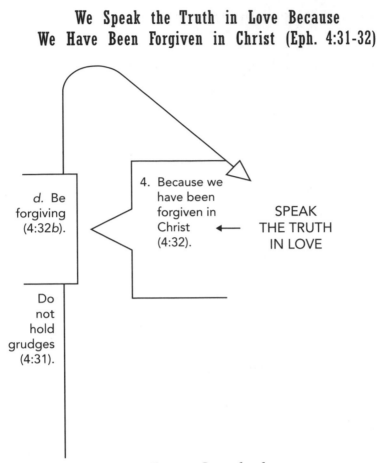

d. Be forgiving (4:32*b*).

Do not hold grudges (4:31).

4. Because we have been forgiven in Christ (4:32).

SPEAK THE TRUTH IN LOVE

Forgive Completely

The command is clear: we are to be forgiving just as Christ forgave us. The verb used in 4:32 implies that through love the barriers to fellowship between persons are set aside. That attitude of "realized forgiveness" describes the climate in the faith community. But what if it is not present? *You* must take the initiative in forgiving regardless of the response of the other person. Realized forgiveness creates a growing desire to build up others in love. It produces a climate in which persons are so close to one another and so confident of acceptance that sharing burdens, forgiving, even taking the other to task is no threat to the relationship. There must be no room for strife, resentment, envy, or any other such thing (v. 31). God's forgiveness enables the Christian to find his or her way back to the one from whom he or she is alienated.

Forgive Quickly

Our forgiveness of others can be immediate or delayed. Paul advised to forgive quickly (4:32). He was influenced by the words of Jesus on the Cross: "Father, forgive them, for they do not know what they are doing" (Luke 23:34). Christ's words didn't change the situation, change the people involved, or reduce the pain He felt. But His words changed things externally. His eternal love didn't allow the words or deeds of others to create within Him bitterness, resentment, and anger—or create a break in the relationship with God the Father.

This principle applies to the servant leader. Withholding forgiveness permits Satan to gain a foothold in our lives (Eph. 4:26-27). Bitterness develops; anger increases; resentment manifests itself externally in leadership decisions or actions. Our calling is to be Christlike even in the uncomfortable situations that often accompany leadership. God will provide inward joy, regardless of the words or deeds of those whom we seek to influence. Paul reminds us that God's grace is sufficient for us *in* our weakness and that His power is made perfect *in* our weakness.

Forgive Proactively

A Christian leader received an e-mail from a person who had angrily left his organization. The former colleague catalogued things done and undone, said and not said. Accusations dotted the communiqué like splotches of ink. The words hurt. The broken relationship was painful. The leader had a decision to make—an immediate, life-changing decision. He replied to the e-mail, taking the initiative to ask forgiveness. And he asked God and the person "wronged" to teach him through this situation. He was proactive in his forgiveness. It's a good model for every servant leader.

Forgive Powerfully

Ephesians 4:25-32 describes a lifestyle by which believers are to live together as the people of God. What happens when they don't? God is grieved (v. 30): "Do not grieve the Holy Spirit of God." Does verse 30 link with verse 29, about "unwholesome talk," or with verse 31, on "bitterness, rage" and so on? The answer is *both*. The Spirit of God is greatly concerned about the speech of His people.

This is a profound theological issue. Anything that tends to destroy fellowship grieves the Spirit who seeks to build it up. The sin of offending a brother by false words or deeds especially grieves God. The Spirit either rejoices or grieves with the words expressed in the fellowship.

Is this *communication lifestyle* possible simply by *human* efforts alone? No, it's not. In 5:18, Paul challenges the people of God with an imperative: "Be filled with [God's] Spirit." Continually. Daily. It is with agape love that the Spirit energizes the believer—living under the sovereignty of the Spirit. Consequently, the faith community is gradually transformed into the image of Christ.

Redemptive Forgiveness

Again, the key question is, "How can we live together as Christians so that our relationships will be redemptive and a witness to unbelievers of the reconciling word of God in Christ?"

Ephesians 4 speaks directly to this issue. (Review Eph. 4:1-3, 11, 15-16, 25, and 5:1-2, 18-21.) We are to "be imitators of God . . . and live a life of love" (5:1-2) in leading and living together as the people of God. We are to model a holiness lifestyle (vv. 1-2). When we do not live like this, we grieve the Holy Spirit. The redemptive forgiveness lifestyle can only be maintained, developed, and strengthened as we are continuously being filled with the Spirit (v. 18).

Consider these questions:

1. Who were the most Christlike leaders you have ever known?
2. What was the spiritual quality that most stands out in your mind?

PURPOSE • • •

5
PREPARING THE BODY OF CHRIST FOR MISSION AND MINISTRY

*The **purpose** of servant leadership is to effectively prepare the Body of Christ—the people of God— for mission and for ministry.*

This principle was at the very core of first-century teaching about discipleship: "And the things you have heard me say in the presence of many witnesses entrust to reliable men who will also be qualified to teach others" (2 Tim. 2:2). And it was the very atmosphere in which the church grew: "They devoted themselves to the apostles' teaching and to the fellowship, to the breaking of bread and to prayer" (Acts 2:42).

Today's social environment has obviously changed. Piety is often shelved in lieu of what is considered the more popular or the more pressing interests. World crises dominate thinking. Economic battles consume the efforts of individuals and families who struggle to make ends meet. Calendars are crowded with recreational and social events. Busyness has taken precedent over blessing. So how do we intentionally nurture personal or corporate spiritual life in order to be effective in both mission and ministry?

Rays of Hope

Thankfully, the rays of a spiritual sunrise are beginning to brighten the horizon. There is an awakening interest churchwide in spiritual disciplines and, more specifically, genuine spiritual formation. Those unfamiliar with the idea should understand that it is the intentional development of the God-you relationship whereby His likeness is being formed in people who seek to know Him intimately. A byproduct of such an endeavor is the ability to understand God's Word in compelling, altering, and challenging ways. There are additional indicators. Many are gathering in small groups, in church communities, or in the workplace for times of intercessory prayer. Christian literature is calling the Christian community to holistic living, with an emphasis on spiritual growth. Another byproduct is the increased sensitivity in the inner ear to hearing and recognizing the still small voice of God.

While these notions may seem lofty and mystical, they are no less a part of *leading Christianly*. It was because Samuel could hear and recognize God's voice that his ministry is so defined in scripture: "The LORD was with him and let none of his words fall to the ground" (1 Sam. 3:19, NRSV).

Engaging the Whole Self

Remember that God is spirit. Christ taught that those who worship Him will worship Him *in spirit* and in truth. He also made you with a soul. This soul in you is a portion of your entire design. The prototype doesn't work without all the elements working in tandem. You are a physical being. You are a cognitive being. You are an emotional being. You are a spiritual being. When God speaks to you, He will communicate to your entire being. Likewise, when you commune with God, you must communicate with your whole self. This is the purpose of the spiritual disciplines, the engagement of the whole self in communion with God—the immersion of the whole self in the supernatural regeneration that is "becoming a new creature in Christ Jesus" (see 2 Cor. 5:17).

Nurturing the Spirit

Abba Arsenius, a well-educated Roman tutor working in a royal household in the fourth century, asked the Lord, "What shall I do to save my soul?" The Lord seemed to respond to his spirit: "Flee, be silent, and pray always." The answers he received apply to our quest as well.

Arsenius and other monks went into the Egyptian desert to escape the spiritual pollution, as they saw it, of the culture. These personal and spiritual experiences of the ancient desert fathers communicate some important principles—specifically in the answers to Arsenius's request for God's guidance, and subsequently to servant leaders.

Flee

"Flee," the Lord said. Arsenius took this to mean that he was to *embrace solitude*. Solitude is a time of inner stillness—aloneness—before God. Finding our "desert" enables us to shift our attention from the things that bring restlessness to God's tranquillity. Jesus personally taught the importance of that instruction in His earthly ministry. In the busyness of ministry to people, Jesus debriefed His disciples and then said in essence, "Let's take a break." Mark 6:30-31 recounts it this way: "The apostles gathered around Jesus and reported to him all they had done and taught. Then, because so many people were coming and going that they did not even have a chance to eat, he said to them, 'Come with me by yourselves to a quiet place and get some rest.'"

Solitude is a quality of the heart—an inner disposition. Profound stillness is not always easy to find. Running off to the Egyptian desert isn't an option for all of us. But we can still find, within ourselves, a place of quiet. Scheduled or spontaneous, we simply say to ourselves, "It's time for a break." The Christian leader knows full well when that R and R is necessary. (And probably those around the leader know it as well!)

Busyness is the enemy of solitude. Quiet before God is imperative for disciples. But that same schedule that has worked against you can be used to draw the boundaries of your own private desert of isolation. Some plan meeting times and dates even as far ahead as a year in advance. Why not plan just as diligently for solitude with God? Visit a retreat center or a monastery in your own quest to find space for God.

Pray, *Speak to me, Lord, regarding my need for times of solitude with You.*

Be Silent

We are a society not only of busyness but also of noise. You only have to wait at the light of an intersection beside a car loaded with a high wattage sound system to understand the problem: Noise is king. Restaurants that once were places of quiet solitude now reverberate with loud music piped into each area by high-powered sound systems. High wattage sound also characterizes modern concerts, Christian or otherwise. Not only does all this noise affect us physiologically, but it also affects us spiritually. Silence is almost nerve-racking to some. The Word of God tells us to be still, to restore our spirits with calm quiet.

The second answer Arsenius heard to his question, "What shall I do to save my soul?" was "Be Silent." We referred to Dietrich Bonhoeffer in chapter 1. In his book *Life Together*,[1] he identifies seven expressions of ministry, including the ministry of listening and of holding one's tongue.

How often we open our mouths and speak about events of the world, about people, or circumstances. How seldom we close our mouths and listen to God and to others within the Body of Christ. Psalm 39:1 says, "I will . . . keep my tongue from sin; I will put a muzzle on my mouth."

We need silence. It is essential for spiritual reading, starting with the Bible.

We need silence. It is essential for spiritual reading, starting with the Bible. Silence is needed for spiritual writing or journaling. Stop asking, "Where will I make the greatest impact or greatest contribution in the Kingdom?" Ask instead, "How can I grow in faithfulness and obedience?" Commit to a new level of consistency with daily prayer. Focus on spiritual alternatives to TV, telephone, and radio. Read devotional classics and books that were written specifically to nurture and strengthen your daily walk with Christ.

Pray, *Speak to me, Lord, regarding my need for silence before You.*

Pray

The Lord said to Arsenius, "Pray always." There are the biblical injunctions to pray *constantly,* pray *unceasingly,* and to *pray always.* How? The following reveal different characteristics of prayer necessary to achieve the instruction Arsenius heard in his heart.

SPEAKING PRAYERS

It is said of the New Testament Church that when they prayed, the place was shaken. That may not just refer to spiritual and sociological changes that resulted from their corporate prayers. It may also refer to people praying out loud—sanctuary praying, conversational prayer, prayer that amplifies the voice of the Spirit over the noise of its surroundings. It is expressed in several ways:

- *Intercessory Prayer*

This is one we are most familiar with. These out-loud, petition-style prayers can be enhanced through the use of a prayer journal, which will be described shortly. Seek to answer the question: What does God want me to do? When we are specific, including "when," "who," "where," and "how" into our prayers, we have a higher percentage of completing the service.

- *Praise—Thanksgiving*

There are wonderful examples of praise and thanksgiving in the psalms. Praise is a functional prayer principle. Psalm 22 tells us God inhabits the praises of His people. When you are praising, you have His attention. Reading the psalms aloud is a way of entering into praise-praying.

- *Reading Prayers*

Prayers can be read from other sources too. Prayer books, such as John Ballie's *The Diary of Private Prayer,* are very helpful. It's not "secondhand prayer." These written expressions of God's communication with His people can be very inspiring—and challenging. Reading about the spiritual growth of another prompts us to grow ourselves.

- *Prayer Journaling*

A typical journal includes a date of entry in one column; specific people and concerns in the second column; and in the third column, specific acts of love, encouragement, and ministries of service.

LISTENING PRAYERS

There are listening prayers. The prophet Samuel prayed, "Speak, for your servant is listening" (1 Sam. 3:10). So should we! Opening the door of the heart and inviting the Holy Spirit to come in and converse with us can be a wonderful experience. Communion isn't always a dialogue. Spiritually, a monologue—with us as the audience—is a rich experience. What does it include?

An expectant heart: "Speak"

A reverent heart: "LORD"

An obedient heart: "your servant"

A focused heart: "is listening"

God will certainly use listening times to plant His divine purpose in your heart.

THINKING PRAYERS

Nouwen says, "To pray, I think . . . means to think and live in the presence of God. . . . What I mean is that we convert our unceasing thinking into unceasing prayer when we move from self-centered monologue to God-centered dialogue."[2] Many pray while they are on the highway—for various reasons. But on-the-go praying is a powerful and purposeful way to let God's thoughts inhabit our thoughts.

LIVING PRAYERS

The most effective way to "pray without ceasing" is to embrace the vision God has for your life. To be a "living sacrifice" (Rom. 12:1) is to engage in living prayer.

Nouwen states, "When I speak of prayer, I refer less to saying prayers than to living a prayerful life in which eating and drinking, sleeping and waking, working and praying are all done to the honor and glory of God."[3]

He continues by quoting a Russian Orthodox monk, who defined prayer as "standing in the presence of God with our mind in our heart."[4]

Pray, *Speak to me, Lord, regarding my need to live with open hands and a life of prayer before You . . . constantly.*

First Things First

In order to "seek first the kingdom of God" (Matt. 6:33, NKJV), we must put first things first. This begins with embracing *solitude, silence,* and *constant prayer.* Consider making an appointment to visit with a spiritual coach or make a regular lunch date with someone who can act as a spiritual father, mother, or accountability partner. Recreation time is meant to refresh the body. Sabbaticals are intended to rest the emotions. Spiritual retreats are designed to recharge the spirit and to reconnect the heart with its Creator. Servant leadership demands that your spirit be healthy and in a right relationship with God. Disciplines drive the leader: proper work habits, boundary setting, time management, physical exercise, mental acuteness, education, and so on. If you neglect the disciplines that strengthen the soul, you will only succeed in handicapping your leadership potential.

PAIN • • •

6

THE PAIN OF SERVANT LEADERSHIP

*The **pain** of servant leadership is experienced when good and godly people collide over visions and values.*

Every now and then it's a good idea to revisit a quote from Teddy Roosevelt, the 26th president of the United States, for encouragement, perspective, and comfort. Reflect on these words:

It is not the critic who counts; not the man who points out how the strong man stumbles, or where the doer of deeds could have done them better. The credit belongs to the man who is actually in the arena, whose face is marred by dust and sweat and blood; who strives valiantly; . . . who knows the great enthusiasms, the great devotions; who spends himself in a worthy cause; who at the best knows in the end the triumph of high achievement, and who at worst, if he fails, at least fails while daring greatly, so that his place shall never be with those cold and timid souls who know neither victory or defeat.[1]

Sometimes the visionary leaders experience the "pain of leadership" when a vision of the future is not accepted or grasped by those for whom the leader is responsible, individuals, it seems to the leader, who often prefer the status quo. Much prayer and the empowering Spirit of God will give the leader the visionary courage, strength, and comfort he or she needs to guide a congregation and a ministry group through necessary (and sometimes painful) transitions.

In teaching emerging leaders, mentors often focus on the joy of leadership and not the pain in leadership. It is true that individuals in leadership positions have the potential to influence change and impact people. This is rewarding and energizing. Leaders are captivated by a vision of growth and expansion—everyone agreeing with them, the world being changed, and all the people showering them with their gratitude!

The gurus don't talk as much about the pain in leadership. This pain can be illustrated by a person standing with outstretched arms. In one hand, the leader holds tenaciously to the vision he or she believes God has given as his or her assignment and responsibility. The individual believes it is the right action to take, policy to adopt, direction to pursue, or goal to attain.

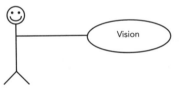

However, from the other extended arm is a hand firmly holding to "reality"—the *situation* or context in which the leader works, the *circumstances* (finances/facilities) that seem to dictate what can and cannot be done, or the *people* or followers who must embrace the vision if what is dreamed is to move from vision to action. And leaders are stunned when those with whom they work reject the vision that is cast or challenge the vision as it is presented.

The tension in holding on to the vision of the future and to the reality of the present situation often produces pain.

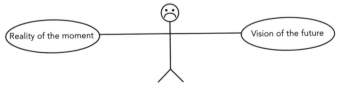

Pain!

If one arm is relaxed and the vision is neglected, the leader drifts along with no direction.

It is in holding, *intentionally,* to both vision and reality that the possibility exists for leaders to move from vision to action, and with this intentionality come both joy and pain for the leader.

Why? Sooner rather than later, Christian leaders are jolted when they experience this reality:

- Good and godly people often differ on how to reach mutually desired goals; and sometimes,
- These good and godly people *collide* . . . and a faith community is divided, the kingdom of God suffers, and Satan laughs.
- This is the *pain* in leadership. Intense pain!

Collisions occur between Christians, not necessarily because of good or bad ideas, noble or sinful goals, or right or wrong solutions. Rather, good and godly people most often collide over *vision* and *values* in the faith community. And the leader is caught in the middle of a divided group of Christians over *where* the group should be going (vision) and *how* they are going to get there (values).

Amid these painful situations leaders often ask themselves these probing questions:

- Applying the question we mentioned earlier, is it possible, in these situations, to live and work *together* as Christians so that our relationships are redemptive and a witness to unbelievers of the *reconciling* work of God in Christ?
- If "in Christ, . . . all things have become new" (2 Cor. 5:17, NKJV), then how does our relationship with Christ inform and guide us in the way we lead in these painful encounters?

- Amid these conflicting situations and irreconcilable expectations placed on us, what does it mean, really mean, to lead a divided faith community with the mind of Christ?

These are good and probing questions—necessary questions.

Moving from Vision to Action

Much can be learned about the leadership qualities needed to guide a faith community when the leader wrestles with the preceding questions. A servant leader learns that moving from his or her vision to action by the entire faith community, particularly in times of conflict and collision, is a lifelong pursuit.

Six "anchors" can hold faithful Christian leaders steady as they grasp firmly to their vision and, at the same time, seek to move the church, university, region, or denomination to action.

Anchor No. 1:	Speak Gracefully
Issue:	"Watch the words."
Principle:	Words spoken can bless or "destroy" people.

- "What comes out of my mouth reflects what is in my heart"—so Jesus states in the Gospels (see Matt. 15:18).
- Leaders
  - Encourage or discourage those with whom they work
  - Uplift or put them down
  - Speak positively or negatively about them
  - Reflect cultural sensitivity or cultural "blindness" to them
  - Focus on the other person or focus on self
- Servant leaders ask themselves, "How do others feel when they leave my presence?"
  - Stronger or weaker?
  - Larger or smaller about themselves?
  - Confident or scared?
  - Understood or misunderstood?

○ Affirmed or manipulated?

○ Blessed or destroyed?

- Guard the temptation to talk more than listen.
- When you speak, make it positive. Listen to the praise to criticism ratio in your conversations! Determine to speak more positively than negatively.
- According to Eph. 4:25, God uses the words spoken to others within the Body of Christ to extend His grace through us to them. What a powerful and probing thought!
- Remember, the words spoken to those with whom we work, especially those who differ and even collide with the leader, can bless them or destroy them. Choose to bless them!

Anchor No. 2:   Live Gratefully

Issue: "Comparison is the root of inferiority."

Principle: Don't whine—be grateful.

- Comparison is so pervasive in our society—in the workforce, the family, the local church or region, in our communities, and particularly within faith communities.
- Christians can feel good about themselves—gifts, talents, and abilities—until they compare themselves with the gifts, talents, and abilities of *other* people.
- Members of a faith community can believe coworkers are adequate for the jobs they give to them until they compare their work—creativity, innovation, energy, collegiality—with others.
- Comparison can eat leaders alive and rob them of joy, relationships, confidence, and peace, and, in the process, sap their energy and drain them of enthusiasm.
- Comparison can transform leaders from being a delightful "boss," supervisor, or pastor into a preoccupied, dejected, negative, and disgruntled individual whom other people only endure.
- What is the antidote to comparison? Three profound biblical qualities:

- ○ Gratitude!
- ○ Thankfulness!
- ○ Appreciation!
- Choose to accept the people and provisions God in His wisdom has given to us.
- Bring out the best in others through seeing the best in them.
- In every situation, choose to be grateful, believing that God is in the midst of all that you are doing (1 Thess. 5:18).
- Gratitude is the "life-giving" antidote to the negative impact of comparison.
- Remember: Don't whine over what you don't have; be grateful—in all things—for what God has provided. Cultivate an attitude of gratitude.

Anchor No. 3: **Listen Intently**
Issue: **"Seek first to understand."**
Principle: **Understanding, not agreement, is the key to conflict management.**

- Believe that good and godly people *can* have honest and intense differences.
- And good and godly people sometimes *collide* over vision and values. You have testimonies to this reality!
- This is why servant leaders must possess a *theological* vision (what you believe about people/what you see in them). Theological vision precedes *organizational* vision (what you want for the church, university, region, or denomination). God can give leaders *His* eyes to really see the people with whom they work.
- In conflict situations with good and godly people, cultivate the art of asking two *growth-producing* questions:
  - ○ "What can I learn?"
  - ○ "How can I change?"
- Likewise, avoid two *growth-inhibiting* questions:

- "Why me?"
- "What if . . . ?"

As a leader you may be a good administrator, however, you *must* be a great *listener*. Leaders can listen for understanding. And listen for what is said. Also, I need to listen for what is not said. Listening to the people with whom you work *values* them. They deserve to be heard. They may have spiritual gifts needed to move the vision to action.

Remember, understanding—not agreement—is the key to conflict management.

Anchor No. 4: **Forgive Freely**
Issue: **"Be proactive in extending forgiveness."**
Principle: **A spirit of forgiveness transforms and empowers leaders.**

- Life's profound leadership lesson is this: forgiveness has little to do with the external environment around me and everything to do with my internal condition!
- Remember this: extending forgiveness does not wait for the "other" to request forgiveness.
- Remember the words of Jesus on the Cross: "Father, forgive them; for they know not what they do" (Luke 23:34, KJV). Was Jesus naive? Did He really believe that those who were killing Him did not know what they were doing? No! Did Jesus believe that by extending forgiveness, those who were slandering Him and hurting Him would cease their activity? No!
- Jesus was not going to permit what others *said* against Him or the evil they *did* against Him to create a bitterness or resentment *within* Him and thereby create a rupture in the relationship with God His Father. It simply was not worth it! "Father, forgive them, they know not what they do!"
- Extending forgiveness frees you from bondage to the other person. Too often, leaders permit persons who have offended us to control us.

- "Great leaders," we are told, "are shaped in the most challenging and difficult times."
- Remember, a spirit of forgiveness transforms and empowers leaders.

Anchor No. 5:	**Lead Decisively**
Issue:	**"Be decisive—avoid paralysis."**
Principle:	**Leaders seldom enjoy the luxury of having all the information they need before making necessary decisions.**

Perhaps you have heard it said that "one person's dream is another person's nightmare!" Yet, it is in this context that leaders live, work, and lead.

- It is in the tension between the *vision* for the future and the *reality* of the present that our decision making as leaders most often takes place. Leaders move between two needs: the need for long-range and strategic planning for our assignments and the daily routine of budgets, personnel, facility management, and interpersonal conflicts. Sometimes this balancing act is between macromanaging (strategy focused on the big picture) and micromanaging (staying focused on the small implementation details of our assignments).
- You want to be a leader of faith and vision, but don't cross the line of irresponsibility. Yet who determines where the "line" really is between *faith* and *irresponsibility*? Leaders don't want to think they have to choose between biblical commands (i.e., "go . . . and make disciples" [Matt. 28:19]) and people needs (i.e., salary increases, equipment needs, and travel expenses). But sometimes they do, and must.
- Always reflect intense respect for brothers and sisters with whom you labor.
- Show respect for your coworkers through
  - The words you speak
  - Expressing gratitude for them
  - Listening to them intently
  - Forgiving freely

- Respecting brothers and sisters in Christ, especially those with whom you differ—even collide with—is at the heart of what it means to "lead with the mind of Christ." However, at some point in our leadership roles, decisions have to be made. The real issue is not *must* a decision be made. Rather, the question is *how*, within the community, decisions are made and implemented.

- Especially in times of conflict over vision, decisions will need to be made—even when continuing differences exist! And in these times, leaders will lead and lead decisively but from their knees and often with a weeping heart.

- Leaders must avoid paralysis—waiting until everyone agrees with them—when decisions must be made. We seldom enjoy the luxury of having all the information we need before making necessary decisions. Sometimes, perhaps often, we must move ahead without everyone within the community agreeing with the vision or direction to be taken.

- How do leaders move ahead, decisively, in these painful situations while, at the same time, show Christian *respect* to those who differ with them? Move ahead—decisively—through
  - *Prayer*, with them, for them, and for you as leader
  - *Collaboration*, involving them when and where you can in the process
  - *Gratitude*, thanking God—and them for their gifts, talents, abilities
  - *And* testimony of faith in Jesus as Lord

- In this spirit of humility and brokenness, leaders move ahead
  - Confidently—believing that God is working in the midst of this difficult situation.
  - Decisively, not with paralysis or uncertainty, but with the conviction that God has spoken His word of vision and direction, and that He will continue to lead His people to action even though the circumstances or attitudes may not give evidence of His work

at the present time. This is leading with the mind of Christ—leading decisively in the midst of complex and difficult situations.

- To lead decisively with Christian humility demands that you continue to nurture and develop
  - Listening and communicating skills
  - Timing and processing skills
  - Affirming and encouraging skills
  - Asking and inquiring skills
  - "Gift" discernment and delegation skills

The more you know about Christian leadership, the more you realize there is to know. Commit yourself to a lifetime of learning what it means to lead decisively with the mind of Christ.

The five anchors discussed thus far to hold you steady as you lead from vision to action are

Speak Gracefully

Live Gratefully

Listen Intently

Forgive Freely

Lead Decisively

Anchor No. 6:	**Love Deeply**
Issue:	**"Value people, not power (or position)."**
Principle:	**The evidence of leadership is seen in the lives of the followers.**

- As leaders, you must keep remembering the many things you have in common with your colleagues and values. Focus on the things that unite you, not the things that divide you.
- Ask yourself often, "Are people stronger in their faith, more confident in themselves, and more fulfilled in their work as a result of working with me as I lead? Do I express appropriate appreciation, thanks, and gratitude regularly to them?"

- Remember to trust your best moments when making decisions about employees. "Let your gentleness be known to all" (Phil. 4:5, NKJV). As leaders, be passionate about communicating your personal and professional (institutional) vision, mission, and values to those with whom you work or for whom you are responsible. Lead the way and encourage them to memorize the strategic vision of the faith community you lead. Talk often about the "overarching priorities of our group." Collectively focus on your core values.

- This is the bottom line: try to enlarge the vision of your people about the work they are doing. Help them see the big picture. Assist them in discovering how they, in their particular assignments, fit into the grand scheme and purpose of the faith community you lead. Value people and progress, not power and position.

- Remember this: the evidence of leadership is seen in the lives of the followers. Servant leaders must never forget that Satan uses discontent and conflict within a faith community to create division and unrest within the fellowship. Stand in the midst of a divided community as a priestly/prophetic/pastoral voice—especially when good and godly people collide over vision and values.

- The "anchors" that have been discussed convict leaders at their worst and characterize them at their best. These "anchors" hold them steady as they seek to move the group for which they are responsible from vision to action.
  - Your words can be grace giving, life generating, and inspiring to others and not discouraging, depressing, and draining utterances.
  - Be known as a person who is forever grateful, regardless of the situation, believing that God is in the midst of everything you do and is working to bring good in every situation.
  - Really listen to and respect the people with whom you work, to understand them—and for them to understand you—even if you do not agree with each other.
  - Initiate forgiveness when you have been offended, because you

don't have the energy or strength to carry the heavy burden and guilt of an unforgiving spirit.

- ○ Lead decisively even as you experience the pain of holding tenaciously to the vision while acknowledging the realities of your situation.
- ○ Believe that your relationship with others will energize them and have a positive impact on their lives. You can enable them, in some small way, to grow—become stronger—in their faith, their confidence in themselves, and their competence at work from their interaction with you in the home and on the job and as their leader.

Yearn to increasingly be a Christian leader in whatever work assignment God gives to you. Discover your own answers—inspired by God's Word and His Holy Spirit to this probing question asked earlier: "If 'In Christ all things are made new,' then how does my relationship with Christ transform and convert the way I lead?"

Remember the three fundamental *convictions* about Christian leadership in a faith community as you wrestle with these issues, questions, and leadership qualities—convictions about

1. *Who* we are as *people* of God
2. *What* we are called to do in the *work* of God
3. *How* we live together as the *family* of God

Jim Collins, in his book *Good to Great*, talks about the critical characteristics of leaders. He speaks of humility and fierce resolve as essential for level 5 or top leaders.[2] Whatever else you discover in Christian leaders, you will find that they

- Speak Gracefully. They watch the words they speak.
- Live Gratefully. They don't whine but are grateful.
- Listen Intently. They seek first to understand.
- Forgive Freely. They are proactive in extending forgiveness.
- Lead Decisively. They avoid paralysis in decision-making with humility.

- Love Deeply. They value people, not power.

Which one of these "anchors" do you need most right now in your leadership assignment? As you experience the tension between the vision God has given you and the reality of your present situation, in which of these areas do you most need God to hold you steady? As you move from vision to action, what is your greatest need? Be specific. Be personal. Be honest.

One more question. Which of these six anchors is your greatest strength? Again, be specific. Be personal. Be honest. It's vitally important for you to affirm your strength even as you acknowledge your need. Build on your strength. Work on your need. Pray for that specific anchor you need and give thanks for the strength God has given you as you lead your people from vision to action.

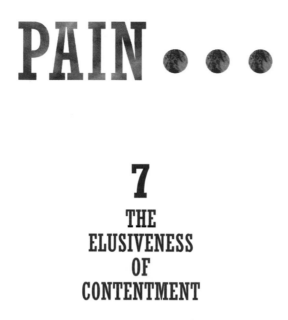

PAIN • • •

7
THE ELUSIVENESS OF CONTENTMENT

When conflicts and collisions occur within the fellowship, the temptation will be to give up and perhaps move on. It is not uncommon for leaders to engage in "pity parties" and complain to God.

During these "feeling sorry for self" times, determine to be content with God's provision for today, and trust with conviction that He will provide what is needed for tomorrow.

But what does it mean to be content? And what is the nature of contentment?

Does it mean that servant leaders must be passive and accept as their duty to God and individuals whatever "darts" and pain come their way? Is contentment the same as fatalism? Does biblical contentment imply a lack of ambition or desire for advancement? Does it mean having no vision of increased leadership responsibilities in a new or old work assignment?

The apostle Paul wrote about the gift of contentment in his letter to the Philippians. For him, contentment is elusive but not impossible to experience, even in the tension of holding tenaciously to a God-given vision while grasping firmly to the reality of the present situation. In the process, contentment as described by Paul will emerge as pivotal and transformative for you. It will hold you steady when you are tempted to run or simply walk away. It is elusive but not impossible to experience.

But why is biblical contentment elusive? To find out, let's examine Paul's guidance in the areas of (1) the irony of contentment, (2) the barriers to contentment, and (3) the secret of contentment. We will find Paul's thoughts and actions especially insightful for the leader in painful situations within a faith community.

The *Irony* of Contentment

- This is the irony: Christians tend to think that they know what is best for their lives, and they ask God for it. (And if God grants their prayers, they will be content!) Philippians 4:4-13 affirms that God can give us inward peace in whatever situation He places us!

- Paul wrote these words on contentment while in prison. The previous two years he had been in another prison near Jerusalem, insulted by the Roman governor of the area, shipwrecked on his way to Rome, without food for 14 days, and then placed in jail when he arrived in Rome! And these seemingly disastrous experiences follow his great teaching and preaching and his three missionary journeys as recorded in the Book of Acts.

- But did Paul moan? Complain? Whine? Blame others for his predicament? Engage in a "pity party"? No! In Rome, while in prison, he did not focus on what he could do if he had more resources, were in another location, worked for a different boss, or had Christian coworkers. He did not focus on "why?" "why me?" or "what if?"

- Instead, while in chains in prison in Rome, Paul wrote what we know as the Prison Epistles: Philippians, Ephesians, Colossians, and Philemon. He "bloomed" where he was planted! And according to Phil. 4:7, God gave to Paul contentment and an inner peace. It's amazingly ironic how tomorrow takes care of itself when we give our best to the workplace and ministry God has given to us today.

- You may not work at the place you prefer, earn the money you desire to earn, have the governing board you desire or the parishioners you believe you need—but in these very situations, ironically, as difficult, unfair, and challenging as they may seem and be, you can experience a contentment that defies understanding.

Biblical contentment is elusive because of the *irony* of contentment. God's ways are not *your* ways.

The *Barriers* to Contentment

- One of the greatest barriers to biblical contentment is comparison. Comparison is the enemy of contentment. Comparison is pervasive—in our educational institutions, among positions at work, regarding the money you earn, the places you live, and even the cars you drive. You can be grateful and thankful for the gifts God has given to you—until you compare your gifts from God to His gifts to others!

- Paul starts at a different point: "I know what it is to be in need, and . . . to have plenty . . . whether well fed or hungry" (Phil. 4:12). And he challenges Christians to do the same and to affirm the appropriate parallels in their lives.

- Comparison in leaders is the root of inferiority. They can feel good about themselves until they compare themselves to others.

- Another barrier to contentment is circumstances. Paul could have said, "Why am I in prison? Why didn't I listen to my friends?" (His friends in the cities of Tyre and Caesarea begged Paul not to continue his journey to Jerusalem knowing that he would face persecution and prison [see Acts 21:3-12].)

  Leaders have these continual temptations:
  - "If I had just listened to . . ."
  - "Life is greener on the other side."
  - "If I were there, I could . . ."
  - "If I had this . . . or that . . ."

  Paul's response to his friends, in Acts 21:14, who begged Paul not to continue to Jerusalem was clear: "The Lord's will be done." And Paul proceeded to Jerusalem and he was at peace.

- Yet another barrier to contentment is people. In any situation, there will be people, and where there are people, there will be problems and possibilities. Will you focus on the problems? Or will you focus on the possibilities?

- In the situation where Paul found himself, he witnessed to many in jail! And as mentioned earlier, he wrote letters to the young churches at Philippi, Ephesus, and Colosse and to Philemon. Paul encourages us to focus on the *possibilities* of our circumstances and not exclusively or morbidly on our problems with the people with whom we live, worship, and work.

We've now seen that biblical contentment is elusive because of the *irony* of contentment and the *barriers* to contentment. But there is a third amazing thought yet to cover:

The *Secret* of Contentment

Biblical contentment is elusive, but it is not impossible to experience. The secret of contentment is not grounded in the people who disappoint you, circumstances that distract you, or problems that overwhelm you. The secret of biblical contentment is grounded in gratitude.

Contentment is rooted in a focus on God and His mercy and grace, not in a preoccupation with people and problems. The foremost quality of a contented person is *gratefulness*.

Listen again to Phil. 4:5-6. "Let your gentleness be evident to all. . . . Do not be anxious about anything, but in everything, by prayer and petition, *with thanksgiving*, present your request to God" (emphasis added). And what is the result? Paul tells us: "And the *peace* of God, which *transcends* all *understanding*, will guard your hearts and your minds in Christ Jesus" (v. 7, emphasis added).

- Gratitude, or "thanksgiving," arises out of your acceptance that *all* of life is grace—as an underserved and unearned gift, a grace gift—from the Father's hand.

- This theocentric, or God-centered, character of gratitude is anchored in ruthless trust that there is a God who is sovereign and whose providential care guides His people.

Contentment does not make you *grateful*. Rather, it is *gratitude* that makes you *contented*. When things go wrong, when people disappoint you, when your colleagues don't understand you, and when it appears that irreconcilable differences exist within the faith community between good and godly people, you can *choose to believe* in the sovereignty of God. In the midst of inner unrest—amid doubts, questions, conflicts, and persecution—you can *choose to believe* in His watchful care over your life.

Choosing to believe like this is often a convictional affirmation, based alone in a radical trust in a sovereign God. When emotions and circumstances do not suggest this affirmation of faith, you can choose to believe in the holy God of grace and mercy to see you through.

- Christians often quote Paul's great statement in Phil. 4:13: "I can do all things through Christ who strengthens me" (NKJV). It is a great verse to remind leaders to be strong and take courage because their faith is in Christ, not themselves or others.
- But this great verse is given by Paul in the context of his discussion of contentment:

  [You] can do *all* things[, whether in need and hungry, or with plenty and well fed—*in either set of circumstances*—you can do *everything* God *wants you to do*] *through Christ who strengthens* [you] *(Phil. 4:13, NKJV, see also vv. 11-12, emphasis added).*

- Whatever the circumstance, or conditions, and regardless of the people—their attitudes and their treatment of you—be grateful for the Christ who dwells within you and gives you contentment in the midst of these difficult situations and circumstances.
- Be grateful—thankful—that in the midst of stress, pressure, and per-

haps misunderstanding, God is teaching you things about yourself, others, life, faith, and trust that you would not—could not—have learned *without* these experiences!

Contentment is grounded in a heart filled with gratitude. Even in prison, the triune God was still in control of Paul's life. Gratitude, for Paul, was not conditioned in good circumstances, understanding employees, pleasant coworkers, or that great salary. Rather, his gratitude was rooted in a ruthless *trust* in the sovereign God of grace and mercy.

Paul challenges God's people to "give thanks"; he teaches you that gratitude is not grounded in murmuring, grumbling, faultfinding, or complaining. Rather, the secret of contentment—for Paul, and for you—is in the conviction that God is *big* enough to handle *any* situation you encounter.

● ● ●

Though there is not much talk about the pain of leadership, it is real, nevertheless. Good and godly people experience clear and intense differences. And you are called to faithfully serve in the midst of these conflicts, even when the differences between visions and values appear irreconcilable.

Paul provides words of guidance for servant leaders. Be content. Live by your faith. "Let your gentleness be known to all" (Phil. 4:5, NKJV).

Don't forget the "six anchors" when leading others in difficult times:

1. Speak Gracefully—watch the words you speak.
2. Live Gratefully—don't whine. Be grateful.
3. Listen Intently—seek first to understand.
4. Forgive Freely—be proactive in lending forgiveness.
5. Lead Decisively—be decisive with humility.
6. Love Deeply—value people, not power.

Give thanks and radiate hope—even in the painful times!

PLAN...

8
LEADERSHIP FOR CONGREGATIONAL TRANSFORMATION

*The **plan** of servant leadership is biased toward spiritual formation and congregational transformation.*

In his book *Servant Leadership* Robert Greenleaf states, "Caring for persons, the more able and the less able serving each other, is the rock upon which a good society is built. Whereas, until recently, caring was largely person-to-person, now most of it is mediated through institutions—often large, complex, powerful, impersonal, not always competent, sometimes corrupt."[1]

He continues, "If a better society is to be built, one that is more just and more loving, one that provides greater creative opportunity for its people, then the most open course is to raise both the capacity to serve and the very performance as servant of existing major institutions by the generative forces operating within them."[2]

When believers adopt a lifestyle of serving, the people of God will build a better society—"one that is more just and more loving," more Christian, and "one that provides" a "greater . . . opportunity for its people." The burden for every local congregation is to "raise both the capacity to serve and the very performance" of a servant.

Modeling the Lifestyle

This improvement will only happen as pastors, board members, Sunday School teachers, youth leaders, nursery workers, ushers, and a host of others in the community of faith model a servant lifestyle. But how do we communicate with each other so that the Christian faith is presented not as an intellectualized belief to be learned but a life to be lived? Is it possible to live together in a community of faith so that "caring for persons, the more able and the less able serving each other," increasingly characterizes the members of the faith community and the local church as a caring institution?

Ephesians 4:11-16 describes such a model. The passage outlines the context, task, goal, dynamic, and purpose for us as Christian leaders in our passion to equip God's people for a lifestyle of service.

THE CONTEXT: "GOD'S PEOPLE" (EPH. 4:11)
THE KEY FOCUS: PARTICIPATION

Since all Christians are called to serve others in Jesus' name, all Christians are also called to educate others in this lifestyle of service. Learning is not limited to students in a classroom. It permeates all the different roles and responsibilities to which we commit ourselves. All of us are on a spiritual pilgrimage and are in the process of becoming what God the Father, Creator, and Redeemer envisions for us.

THE TASK: "PREPARE GOD'S PEOPLE" (EPH. 4:12)
THE KEY IDEA: FORMATION

Christian formation, or preparing God's people, means enabling the individual to grow in Christlikeness. This demands

- An acquaintance with the Christian tradition
- An awareness of world issues
- Development of personal faith
- Competence in vocational skills
- A Christian worldview
- A global perspective

- Growth in community life

Further, we need guidance in developing a lifestyle of devotion to Christ, in caring for the world, nurturing our own spiritual lives, relating to other world citizens, developing personal qualities, and inculcating values by which we live and die.

THE GOAL: "WORKS OF SERVICE" (EPH. 4:12)
THE KEY THOUGHT: EXPRESSION

Our "works of service," or mission, is a function and expression of the entire church. Our goal is to prepare God's people to participate in this mission, which is to proclaim the kingdom of God, nurture the people of God, and serve the whole human community. We must be captured by this vision. This means transcending service *to* the people and *for* the people, to service *with* the people and *by* the people.

THE DYNAMIC: "LOVE WITHIN THE BODY OF CHRIST" (EPH. 4:15-16)
THE KEY CONCEPT: INTERACTION

Interaction is defined as an intimacy of relationship between members within the Body of Christ. In every New Testament passage where the Body of Christ is discussed, there is a relational setting in which this kind of mutual nurturing takes place. Passing on information does not produce a servant of Christ. Trust needs both to be explained and demonstrated in the setting of an intimate relationship. Love and trust free us to know and reveal ourselves to one another—modeling, rather than indoctrinating, is the method of leadership for lifestyle change.

THE PURPOSE: TRANSFORMATION FOR A "HOLINESS LIFESTYLE" (EPH. 4:13)
THE KEY ISSUE: CHRISTLIKENESS

The purpose of Christian leadership is to participate with God in the reconciling and transforming of humankind, by grace. This is so that holy people may be equipped for a Christlike ministry of service to others, as they fulfill their vocational responsibility. This is also true in the congregational setting. A holiness lifestyle focuses on the progressive transformation of the Christian toward the character, values, motives, attitudes, and understanding of God himself.

Developing Character

Dr. Francis Hesselbein said, "Leadership is about who you are, not what you do." Some know what they want to *do* with their life. But they fall short in their vision of what they want to *be*—until they are changed by radical faith in Christ. Servant leaders not only have experienced that radical faith but also are ultimately motivated to lead people into its discovery.

Regardless of where you are on your spiritual journey, God is pursuing you. His vision for us is that we become "men and women of good and godly character" (see 2 Pet. 3:11-12). D. L. Moody once wrote, "If I take care of my character, my reputation will take care of itself."

Character is different from reputation. William Davis highlights the difference:

> Reputation is what you are supposed to be; character is what you are. Reputation is what you have when you come to a new community; character is what you have when you go away. Your reputation is made in a moment; your character is built in a lifetime. Reputation makes you rich or makes you poor; character makes you happy or makes you miserable. Reputation is what men say about you on your tombstone; character is what the angels say about you before the throne of God.[3]

A tiger trap for many in leadership is to secure and promote a saleable reputation. Reputations make or break careers and opportunities. But what you need to be cultivating is your character. Sometimes the border between these two concepts is a dotted line. How can you know if your focus is centered on character rather than reputation? Let me ask you some questions, and your answers will distinguish the difference.

- Who are your heroes?
- What do you read?
- How do you spend your free time?
- What do you watch on TV or at the movies?

- Are your words spoken to and about others upbuilding or undermining, encouraging or discouraging, truth or gossip?
- How close to the edge are you living?

Character is imperative. It is who you are when no one else is around. Character isn't just who you are when you're making a presentation, preaching, or teaching a seminar. It's also who you are when you're late to that presentation, on the side of the highway with a flat tire. It's not only who you are when others are showering thanks on you for Christmas gifts but also who you are when you were untangling the Christmas lights. Who are you in the times of pressure? Character springs from the core values from which you build your life.

Moral Compass

You lead and serve in a world that needs direction—in a world that has lost its way morally and spiritually. God's vision is to provide you with a moral compass. The advice of His Word, the guidance of His Spirit, and the counsel of His children is God hasn't abandoned your need for direction. He's even given you a list of character traits. Second Peter 1:5-7 includes those qualities:

Faith

Goodness

Knowledge (or discernment)

Self-control

Perseverance

Godliness

Brotherly kindness

Love

Be careful. It's easy to be dragged down by your failures or the failures of others. People are difficult to work with—and for. Many character traits that are the opposite of the biblical model can develop over time, including a cynical tongue, a judgmental spirit, a negative attitude, a condescending demeanor, manipulativeness, deceptiveness, or immoral behavior.

If we do not guard our thoughts and spirit, these negative attitudes and actions will eat us alive. More important than the habits of effective people are the character qualities they passionately pursue. Paul's list in Eph. 4:2 includes humility, gentleness, patience, and kindness. The Old Testament prophet Micah gave us a stirring question-answer: "And what does the LORD require of you but to do justly, to love mercy, and to walk humbly with your God?" (6:8, NKJV).

Leadership by Leading

You have a responsibility to be a role model, enabling and encouraging others in building their character. This will usually happen while leading others, and particularly in developing their leadership skills. They will be watching you, even as they are listening to you. Your character will influence theirs. In this mentoring process, you ought to be aware of the potential mistakes leaders make. Discussions often take place around these frequent mistakes of a leader:

Mistakes	Necessary Alternatives
Inconsistency	Consistency
Indecisiveness	Decisiveness
Duplicity	Integrity
Reactive	Proactive
Dishonesty	Honesty
Impure motive	Pure motive
Sloth	Tenacity
Flighty	Dependable
Talks too much	Listens before speaking
Disloyalty	Loyalty

A Christian leader—a servant leader—will do a periodic "flight check," asking two important questions: (1) Has my faith been strengthened or weakened as a result of my work? (2) In what ways do my spiritual gifts match the responsibilities that have been assigned to me? Modeling is the primary method or process by which leaders pass on the fundamental character qualities and values needed in future leaders.

The Holy Calling

God's vision for you is that you become someone who lives a holy life. Good and godly character isn't accidental; it is intentional—it must be developed in our lives. Second Peter 1:3 tells us that what God calls us to, He equips us for: "[God's] divine power has given us everything we need for life and godliness." Our job? In verse 5, we are challenged to "make every effort to add to [our] faith [these qualities]." In other words, the character qualities identified by Peter flow from a life that has been saved by God's grace alone, through faith in Jesus Christ, who calls us to a life of holy living—on purpose.

The Blessing of Brokenness

The attributes of a holy life must be nurtured, cultivated, and developed if we are going to become like Christ. Christian character formation takes place over a lifetime and is shaped through our responses to scriptural imperatives and through a process of brokenness and prayer. There is a painful yet fascinating relationship between brokenness and character development. Continually ask the question in the conflict situations of life, "What does God need to teach me about my character through this circumstance or through this encounter?"

In the book *Becoming a Person of Influence* the authors say, "Many succeed momentarily by what they know, some succeed temporarily by what they do, but few succeed permanently by who they are."[4] Five questions will help you along in a lifelong pursuit of Christian character development:

1. Will this action strengthen me spiritually?
2. Would I want my child, my spouse, or my best friend to copy this action?
3. Does this action violate a biblical principle?
4. Does this action strengthen the Body of Christ?
5. Would an unbelieving friend be attracted to Christ and the Christian faith by my behavior?

A Godly Beginning

Godly character development begins with the new birth. Nicodemus asked Jesus how to begin a quest for a righteous character—a holy and godly life (John 3:1-8). Notice that he might have had an edge on the question:

Nicodemus had an excellent reputation.

He belonged to the strictest religious group of the day.

He observed the law.

He fasted regularly.

He prayed often.

He paid a tithe of his income.

He was a member of the Sanhedrin.

He was one of the 70 elders who governed the religious and social life of the people.

He had authority and prestige.

He was educated, well off, and respected in the community.

But Jesus "lowered the spiritual boom" when He gave him the primary qualification: "You must be born again" (see v. 3). It wasn't about Nicodemus' reputation; it was about his relationship. Godliness begins with a relationship with God through faith in the Lord Jesus Christ. When a person is "born again," that person is born anew by the Spirit of God—alive, now, to spiritual truth.

If you haven't done so already, reach out and take what God is trying desperately to give you—a new nature. As a child of God, partake in the holiness of God. The result is a radical change of divine design in conduct and character.

Second Corinthians 5:17 says, "If anyone is in Christ, he is a new creation; the old has gone, the new has come!" This is more than just patchwork, or outward reformation. This is an inner, moral transformation. The new birth, or new life in Christ, is a mystery because it is a miracle of God. "God was in Christ reconciling the world to Himself" (v. 19, NKJV). Christ took your sin upon himself and died in your place. He did for you what you could not do for yourself. So the question is, How will you respond to what

God has done? Will you choose to embrace a radical faith or remain in disbelief?

Maybe you're still living on your reputation. If so, then you're still wading in the shallow end of the faith pool. When you complete your present ministry assignment, will you be remembered more for your spiritual character than for your vocational reputation?

Do you know that you've been born again by the Spirit of God? Has Christ's *character* been formed in you by your surrender to His will? You can be sure of your relationship with Christ. First, ask Him to forgive you for the sins that you have committed. Second, believe that He came to save you and that He can save you now. Third, confess Him as Lord of your life, your Savior, and your Redeemer. Fourth, decide that you want His life—His character—to be shaped in you. Fifth, thank Him for finishing the job! God is waiting to enable and empower you to be just exactly the person He envisioned when He created you.

The Leader as Catalyst

Remember it is the Holy Spirit that teaches us—by our developing the skills He has entrusted to us and listening for His further instruction. Our responsibility as spiritual leaders is to first look to God in worship and devotion; we need to *reach up* to seek God's wisdom and His guidance before we *reach out* to others. After seeking His will in prayer and in His Word, plan accordingly.

The specific tasks of planning include assessing our congregations' needs, clarifying our ministry and mission, determining programs, and establishing goals. Here are some key questions to ask:

- Who are we?
- Where are we now?
- Where are we going?
- Why?

Have a Clear Vision

Clarifying your mission will help you set appropriate goals. That's nothing new. In fact, it's become cliché. But the reason you keep hearing it is because too often "the ball of planning" gets dropped. The led haven't "bought into" the direction of the leader. They don't clearly understand what he or she expects of them—and where they are expected to go as individuals or as a team.

Communicate the Vision

A clear vision empowers you to explain your organizational purpose to those with whom you will be working. Knowing the "purpose" helps to focus group energy more effectively. Often the why questions are unanswered in order to withhold power or curtail conflict, disagreement, or discussion. But in Proverbs it says, "Where there is no vision, the people perish" (29:18, KJV).

Picture leaders in your mind. Think about how God sees them:

People of God?

A community of faith?

The Body of Christ?

The fellowship of the Spirit?

A Spirit-led and Spirit-filled people?

A ministering people—called, gifted, trained, and sent?

A growing people?

What does that mean to you? Now imagine the faces of those who look to you for leadership. (Yes, even the ones who cause you grief.) Name them, as God does. See your constituents in your mind, personally and corporately, and call them by the name you envision God has given them: "These are the people of God." "This is my community of faith." "They are the Body of Christ." As such, they deserve a clear mission. They deserve every opportunity to succeed.

Organize! Strategize! Execute!

Once the vision is clear and your mission set, it is important to organize the process. The task is to implement the vision. Questions to ask are, "How will we get there?" and "When will we get there?"

Put deadline dates on each part of the process. You will have a much higher probability of completing your goal, if there is a date attached with it. Organizing the goals and determining when they are to be completed will give you a map or a structure to the process. It will help keep you and your congregation on track.

Become a good motivator. The task is to mobilize your congregation to complete the agreed-upon goals. Determine who will be responsible for each part of the process or plan. Remember that motivation is more than generating enthusiasm. It is teaching. It is equipping. Motivating others is critical. The work that God has for us is too big to be done alone. Ideally you will become a spiritual talent scout, helping others recognize their calling and their gifts in order to train them.

Evaluate

Another leadership requirement is being a good evaluator. This involves reviewing the process, acquiring feedback, and changing the process or structure or deadline if changes need to be made to complete the goals. Typical questions are, "Were we successful?" "What needs improvement?" "Where are we?" "When do we make changes?" "How do we best use this information?"

The motivating force is optimism. By assessing where the ministry team is and how they are doing, you can celebrate the successes as each intermediate goal is reached. Evaluating also provides a baseline to compare with as you instigate other programs, processes, benchmarks, and baselines. The graph on the following page shows how the functions of a leader can be used to facilitate congregational transformation.

The Dynamics of Christian Leadership

True leadership always happens on purpose. And that purpose comes from the heart of a visionary—one who believes that God "is able to do immeasurably more than all we ask or imagine, according to his power that is at work within us" (Eph. 3:20). Vision births vision. A Christian leader who sets the course will have people who will follow. It's a proven dynamic. But how is the vision transferred?

THE LEADER AS CATALYST FOR CONGREGATIONAL TRANSFORMATION

LEADERSHIP FUNCTIONS	THEOLOGICAL PERSPECTIVES	KEY QUESTIONS	SPECIFIC TASKS	ORGANIZATIONAL CONCERNS
DREAMING AND PLANNING	The People of God The Community of Faith The Body of Christ The Fellowship of the Spirit	Who are we? Where are we now? Where are we going? Why?	Clarify vision and mission Assess congregation Determine program Establish goals	Purpose
ORGANIZING AND ADMINISTERING	A Spirit-led and gifted people	How will we get there? When will we get there?	Organization and Implementation	Structure
MOTIVATING AND INSPIRING	A Ministering People Called, Gifted Trained, Sent	Who will be responsible?	Mobilization and Energizing	Personnel
EVALUATING AND ENCOURAGING	A Growing People	Were we successful? What needs improvement? Where? When? How?	Review Feedback Encouragement Change	Organization Dynamics and Processes

Shaping a Reconciling and Transforming Ministry Through

Reaching Up	←	Worship/Devotion
Reaching Out	↑	Witness/Service/Evangelism
Reaching In	↓	Christian Nurture/Spiritual Formation
Reaching Around	↺	Fellowship/Community/The People of God

Define It

Vision is defined as "the ability to see clearly and at a great distance." The mountain climber, about midway up the rock, somewhere between exhaustion and exhilaration, has to answer the question, "Why?" The same question will be asked in your organizational "mountain climbing." You will find yourself waging wars you want no part of and finishing fights you did not pick. When the way gets rough and challenges are formidable, your only lifeline will be found in knowing what's ahead, how to get there, and why you settled on the choices you made.

As a Christian servant leader, life is lived with Christ as your identity, Christ as your motivator, Christ as your mission writer, Christ as your navigator, and Christ as your source of provision. The Cross defines your vision. Your life frames purpose and meaning through the perspective of the Kingdom.

Remember that leadership is the transference of vision. Without vision, no creative work of significance has ever come to birth. Vision (spiritual imagination) is the fuel through which information is converted into creative energy. It rules the universe of great events.

Fundamental to Christian leadership is a theological vision. Seeing what others do not see brings to focus a consuming, passionate, compelling inner picture. A theological vision for motivating the people of God for mission and ministry!

Build It

To build a vision you might ask these questions:

- If you knew you couldn't fail, where would you like to be five years from now?
- What if?
- Why not?

Communicate It

A vision tells the world what the organization is, how it will operate, how it will deal with its stakeholders—both internal and external—and what values and principles it will attempt to live out as it pursues its ministry assignment. Vision channels values into the work environment and becomes a word picture of how those values are to be lived out.

Vision statements foster "winning" consciousness. They express optimism and hope. They are more than a dream of what the organization is to be like. They are its mold; its template of what the Kingdom-driven ministry *will become*. Like the plates for new money, the vision statement is more than a shadow in the back of someone's mind; rather, it is the physical, tangible expression of what will soon become a reality. You can see and touch what currency will be. Vision is the herald of things amazing and imminent.

Passion, energy, enthusiasm, optimism, faith—these leadership dynamics fuel vision. Robert Kennedy, rephrasing the words of George Bernard Shaw, said, "Some men see things as they are and say why; I dream things that never were and say, why not?" Dr. Robert Jarvik, inventor of the Jarvick-7 artificial heart, once said, "Leaders are visionaries with a poorly developed sense of fear and no concept of the odds against them."

Personalize It

Don't overlook *your* personal vision and mission. For example, your mission may include being a Christian role model and leader to your family first and subsequently to your vocational responsibilities—in the context of servant and visionary leadership. Giving attention to the financial needs of your family, including retirement, and keeping yourself physically and emotionally conditioned will enable you to function with maximum effectiveness.

You are a growing professional who must give priority time to strategic planning for the organization you serve. Your mission, then, has the added responsibility of enabling and energizing your family, friends, and colleagues to give their best to their unique roles and assignments. All servant-leader activities initiate from and operate out of a pastoral call—as a follower of Jesus who endeavors to articulate, model, and always be committed to His life and teachings.

Developing theological, organizational, and personal vision statements take time. If you have not already done so, get away and begin the process. Give yourself several months for this *transforming* experience. And be sure to share the draft statement with someone you trust.

Grow It

In the tall shadows of a leadership giant, the rookie leader Joshua inherited the position of Moses and led the people of Israel with a heart for God and a big vision: "Be strong and courageous" (Josh. 1:6). He also faced a company of naysayers along the way.

As mentioned earlier, sometimes the visionary leader experiences the "pain of leadership" when a vision of the future is not accepted by the led. People often prefer the status quo. There's a reason we use the word "familiar." Its root is in the word "family." The things we are accustomed to become *normal*. For example, dysfunctional families often have no clue that they are operating in dysfunction. It's been "familiar" for so long, it just seems right.

Chapter 5 advised that prayer and the empowering Spirit of God can give a leader the visionary courage, strength, and comfort needed to guide a ministry group through transitions. But there is a tendency to disregard this advice. Even among those who lead Christian and spiritual organizations, prayer often sounds like a hokey cop-out—a last resort for those who have nowhere to look but up. This couldn't be further from the truth. The fact is, if prayer seems like a call to an ineffectual "spiritual coffee break," it is time to put this book down and rediscover your Heavenly Father. Understand that God is calling you to a deeply personal relationship with Him.

He has never called you to do things *for Him*. Yes, you are capable. And you may enjoy building organizational castles. But remember that God has equipped you with valuable (and recognized) skills in leadership and management. That is why you are reading this book. Someone has entrusted you with the stewardship of God's own.

Capability is not enough. Availability is more important. Until you know Him—in His eternal wisdom and power—you cannot effectively serve Him. The Bible suggests that all of our building is in vain unless the Lord is the Contractor (see Ps. 127:1).

Transition Curve

Understanding transitions is important for the leader. Transitions in the church or institution you serve are inevitable The questions for church leaders are these:

Do congregations (and individuals) go through numerical (and spiritual) cycles?

Are the cycles inevitable?

How do they regain momentum in the midst of cycles?

Most transitions follow a "curve" that includes a point of initiative—someone has a dream, then comes the time of resourcing the vision—you slow down to resource the dream. Growth usually takes place and the vision takes hold. The organization becomes effective and efficient.

It is during this "prime" time that a new vision is required. Otherwise decline begins when the same things are done as in earlier years. It is during the time of growth—not when the church or organization is declining—that leaders must dream new dreams with the people they serve. Regarding the time of pausing to reflect on the growth that has taken place, the leader must ask, "What are the 'old endings' that must go?" and "What are the core values of the 'old' that must be retained?"

Regarding the transition period, the leader's role is to articulate the "end" vision but retain core convictions. The leader during this period of change and transition must model consistency, steadiness, integrity, respect, trust, and communication.

Regarding new beginnings, the leader must engage the people in institutionalizing the transition through which they are going and toward which they are moving. The leader must continue to model the Christian character qualities of Eph. 4 and 1 Pet. 1, especially in conflict situations and with congregational members who differ with him or her.

There is a critical time when the pastor and the local governing board have the responsibility to start a new curve. Here are a couple more questions for pastors:

1. Where is your congregation in the cycle?
2. What should be the role of pastoral leadership in this cycle?

You serve a great God who has given you a great assignment: enabling others to fulfill their ministry to each other and their mission in the world in the context of a dynamic laboratory of learning.

PLAN...

9

PERSONAL TRANSFORMATION AND SPIRITUAL LEADERSHIP

What drives a commitment to spirituality in leadership? What manifests itself in the preparation of the faith community for personal spiritual formation and congregational transformation? According to Dr. John Bowling, it is *grace-fullness.*

It is the antithesis to the arrogant, self-centered, and self-dependent leadership that is manifest in such descriptions as, "That guy is full of himself." Servant leaders aren't full of themselves; rather, they are full of Christ. His attitude is imprinted on their lives, and His compassion is primary to their purpose. In Bowling's book *Grace-Full Leadership: Understanding the Heart of a Christian Leader,* he outlines the characteristics of such a leader. These are their qualities:

- They "are more concerned with spirit than style."
- They "are covenantal rather than contractual."
- They "view people as ends — not means."
- They "recognize the changeable from the changeless."
- They "seek significance, not just success."
- They "are responsive as well as responsible."
- They "are high-touch."

- They "maximize influence and minimize authority."
- They "are passionate."
- They "focus primarily on the body, not the head."

These are their traits:

- They "understand accountability."
- They "interact rather than react."
- They "follow their 'knows.'"
- They "are willing to follow as well as lead."
- They "maintain their balance."
- They "have double vision."
- They "go deep."
- They "are skilled meteorologists."
- They "anticipate through planning, pathfinding, planting, and prospecting."
- They "take care."[1]

It would be wise for us to use those qualities and traits as a catalyst for our further study of transformational leadership—personal transformation that results in organizational transformation. We reflect again that in Christian leadership (servant leadership) "who we are" impacts "what we do" and "where we are going."

No earthly leader exemplified that any more than the Savior. From His childhood ("'Why were you searching for me?' he asked. 'Didn't you know I had to be in my Father's house?'" [Luke 2:49]) to His earthly ministry ("I have brought you glory on earth by completing the work you gave me to do" [John 17:4]) to His last message ("When he had received the drink, Jesus said, 'It is finished.' With that, he bowed his head and gave up his spirit" [19:30]), Jesus lived from the inside out. "The Word became flesh and made his dwelling among us. We have seen his glory, the glory of the One and Only, who came from the Father, *full of grace and truth*" (1:14, emphasis added).

And from that wellspring, every Christian leader may draw. "From the fullness of his grace we have all received one blessing after another" (v. 16).

And what's more, from that source every Christian leader *must* draw! There are too many steep hills, too many sharp turns, and too many construction zones for anyone to depend on anything but the fullness of God's grace in leading citizens of this world to fulfill their heavenly mission and ministry.

Let's use Bowling's list of characteristics for the grace-full leader to summarize the important qualities and traits of servant leadership.

Grace-Full Leaders Are More Concerned with Spirit than with Style

A grace-full leader has the right combination of confidence and humility to recognize strengths and weaknesses and to consciously seek to build character, competency, and the confidence of those who are led. This formula is a key component of leadership. Leadership is the tapestry of integrity of heart and life, words and deeds, thoughts and actions.

Grace-Full Leaders Are More Concerned with Covenantal Rather than Contractual Relationships

Contracts take the place of trust; covenants express it, for trust is at the heart of a covenantal relationship. While most relationships have some elements of both, at some point all relationships become essentially one or the other. Contractual relationships exist because of what people *do* for each other. Covenantal relationships exist because of what people *are* or *mean* to each other.

Grace-Full Leaders View People as Ends—Not Means

While occasionally within organizational life things do change and people are displaced, nonetheless, the grace-full leader seeks to foster an environment where people can flourish. Leadership that does not promote the overall welfare of the people involved might appear to be efficient and powerful, but it is not Christian. Grace-full leaders recognize the dignity of others and affirm the diversity of their gifts.

Everyone comes with certain gifts—but not the same gifts. A polar bear is as unique as a stingray, but don't ask a polar bear to survive under water or a stingray to survive on polar ice. The leader's challenge is to match the person to the position and need at any given time.

Grace-Full Leaders Recognize the Changeable from the Changeless

Personal change can be a genuine opportunity for renewal, but the problem is the "change has no constituency." That is to say, most people do not like change. Change often means letting go of things that are familiar and moving into unknown territory. Even when a person does not like things as they are, he or she may still find it hard to venture into the unknown. To successfully determine what should change and what should not, and then to effectively manage those things, you must first be comfortable with the realities of change in your own life. If the followers are to respond positively, the leader must first accept the pace and necessity of change.

Grace-Full Leaders Seek Significance, Not Just Success

In the New Testament it becomes clear that although we must work, our primary calling (vocation) is to repentance, faith, fellowship, and service. Men and women are called to be new creations in Christ. This call *to be* precedes the call *to do*. The Bible doesn't indicate that God "calls" us to an earthly profession or trade. Paul, for example, was called by God to be an apostle; he was not called to be a tentmaker, as shared by Elton Trueblood in *Your Other Vocation*.[2]

So faith makes a difference in how one views work and how one works. Bringing the gospel to all of life can flood a person's working hours with new meaning and new potential. The hours spent at work can become "Kingdom hours" that provide a powerful witness to the world of the grace and glory of God. It is vital to the church, the individual, and the world at large that a true integration of faith and work take place in the life of every believer. As this happens, success gives way to significance.

Grace-Full Leaders Are Responsive as Well as Responsible

Being responsive allows an organization to discontinue practices no longer effective. Most good ideas and effective methods run their course in time and need to be replaced with other good ideas and effective methods. The "we've always done it that way" attitude is often hard to overcome because the weight of tradition and organizational history supports the tried-and-true ways of the past. The responsive leader has the ability to recognize when new outcomes are needed and when old methods may not be sufficient.

Grace-Full Leadership Is "High-Touch"

In at least four dimensions, grace-full leaders "reach out and touch." *First*, they are in touch with themselves internally. They know what makes them tick—and how to keep their inner "workings" in sync with the Spirit. *Second*, they are in touch with the internal and external environment in which they must function. Their heads are buried in the sands of society. But at the same time, they are not subjects to that society. They are informed but not engrossed with the world around them. *Third*, they are in touch with those whom they lead. They take the time to know their colleagues on a human level, rather than on a leader-led level. They make every effort to express concern and compassion for those they lead. *Fourth*, and more importantly, they are in touch with God. To them, He is not a "go-to God." Rather, He is a constant Companion and Counselor; both Lord of the universe and Lord of their heart.

Grace-Full Leaders Maximize Influence and Minimize Authority

Whenever possible, grace-full leaders seek to lead through influence rather than authority. The difference between the two approaches strikes at the heart of why and how employees/members/followers choose to respond to leadership initiatives. If the only method of motivation is the authority of the leader, the response of the follower will no doubt be a minimal commitment. The follower may comply with his or her hands but not with the head or heart.

Grace-Full Leaders Are Passionate

Leaders have tenacity and perseverance, as well as courage and energy. We would like for all our work to be exciting and immediately rewarding, but it isn't always that way; much of life and labor is tough and boring and routine, and therein lays the challenge to excellence. For grace-full leaders, merely repeating Jesus' words is not to continue His work; they must be intent on reproducing His life and passion. Such leaders are not building their kingdoms, but His; grace-full leaders are passionate people, set aflame by the Spirit.

Grace-Full Leaders Focus Primarily on *the Body*, Not the Head

Leaders focus on people, not position. A spirit of community within the Body of Christ doesn't just happen; it must be fashioned and fostered, nourished and maintained. Community can be a fragile thing in many ways. Relationships can be broken, isolation can set in, and communication can dissipate. Employees and coworkers can drift apart, living in their own little worlds, almost untouched by the others. Leadership that has a personal agenda does not foster an environment that reaches corporate goals.

Grace-Full Leaders Understand Accountability

Accountability means that leaders take responsibility for their words and actions. And just as one is accountable *to* others, the grace-full leader is also accountable *for* others. Leaders must bear a sense of responsibility for the individuals with whom and for whom they work. Leaders often are called upon to balance the needs of people and of the organization. Consequently, they must submit an "organizational balance sheet" to those to whom they are responsible—whether a person or a board of directors.

Grace-Full Leaders Interact Rather than React

Interactive leadership is a recognition that we may legitimately act in different ways at different times, depending on the interaction we have with the circumstances confronting us. Management is both a science and an art. This is the *art* part. It is a way to maximize our timing and to learn from the environment as we plan our proactive and reactive responses. Consensus that leads to constructive ministry comes from a pool of talented resources, rather than an exclusive and personal view of the mission or ministry.

Grace-Full Leaders Follow Their "Knows"

Following your "knows" involves getting the right information, talking with the right people, and balancing that input with your instincts and inner compass—but there is more. Ultimately, for the Christian leader, knowing must also include the spiritual dimension. God has promised wisdom and guidance, protection and empowerment. The grace-full leader knows that he or she must stay in tune with God and follow His leadership. Of all the things there is to know, knowing God is most important.

Grace-Full Leaders Are Willing to Follow as Well as Lead

A "leader who follows" might, at first glance, appear to be an oxymoron. However, the grace-full leader knows that learning to follow is one of the first great lessons of leadership. This idea of leaders as followers may take some getting used to for some. It seems just the opposite of the natural role of leadership, which is commonly understood as being out front, pointing the way, and giving the orders.

Grace-Full Leaders Maintain Their Balance

Leaders walk a higher and more precarious tightrope than a high-wire acrobat. The only similarity is that both are under the scrutiny of the audience. Balance in life prevents becoming an extremist or being eccentric in beliefs, attitudes, and actions. It keeps the pressures of success and failure in proper balance. Dealing with adversity and prosperity are two extreme tests. Both challenge your ability to remain steady and focused and to keep spiritual equilibrium. And of the two, perhaps success is the hardest.

Grace-Full Leaders Have Double Vision

Leadership demands that you see both *what is* and *what can be*. This "double vision" helps to enable us to keep our sights set on the future, as we deal with the daily demands of leadership. Christian leadership is like playing Twister. The leader must have two hands on the "dots of the present," while one foot is planted on the "dot of the past" and another on the "dot of the future." But the most immediate need is to focus on the present and the future. The past serves as a guide to both.

Grace-Full Leaders "Go Deep"

Grace-full leaders know that having wet feet rather than cold feet means they must be willing to take those first steps of leadership. No matter how unlikely the timing or difficult the circumstances or impossible the task, it falls to the leader to lead. In two instances of his discipleship, Peter (the fisherman turned apostle and the apostle that temporarily turned fisherman) experienced the "go deep" concept. In the first, the apostle was the only one in the boat to step out and take a courageous step toward the Master (Matt. 14:27-30). In the other, he took a bold vocational step following the Crucifixion. Following a futile night of fishing (that didn't include catching any fish), Peter responded to the instruction of Jesus, shouted from the shoreline. He broke tradition and cast his net on the other side of the boat (John 21:1-6).

Grace-Full Leaders Are Skilled Meteorologists

Every organization has a "climate." A skilled leader knows how to react to various organizational weather patterns—storms, calm, high pressure, thunder, and lightning. Leadership is, in many ways, a foul-weather job because that's when a leader is most severely tested. One cannot always avoid the winds, the snow, and the sleet, but a leader can prepare for them. Anticipating the storm is one key responsibility of a leader.

Grace-Full Leaders Anticipate Through Planning, Pathfinding, Planting, and Prospecting

Good leaders create positive energy that helps people overcome obstacles, break free from inertia, and rise to new challenges and levels of performance. They act in the present with the future in mind—they anticipate. Their blueprint isn't more important than their Bible, but they know it has its place—and should always be in its place. Leaders cut the brush of new trails—making the way clearer for those who follow.

Grace-Full Leaders Take Care

Grace-full leaders learn to take care of their relationship to God, themselves, and their organizations. Unless care is consistently given to each aspect of life, a person's leadership can be eroded. Grace-full leaders are aware that an organization is held together by shared values, beliefs, and commitments. This is what gives it fiber, integrity, and the capacity to endure cyclical hardships. Since organizations are people, the first way to care for the organization is to hire the right people—individuals who are committed to the core values of the organization. One of leadership's classic axioms is to "hire for attitude and train for skills."

Learning to lead is a lifelong process. It doesn't happen by just reading a book or simply taking a course of study. We all learn to lead by leading. And learning to lead is also a part of learning to live—with purpose and meaning beyond our own interests and abilities. The world is waiting for a new generation of leaders—men and women whose mission is more than profit, whose morality is not contextual, and whose very life is an expression of grace; leaders who will manage themselves, inspire others, and forge the future.

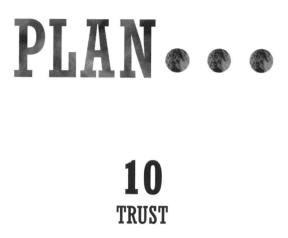

10
TRUST

"Opinion polls don't count for much, do they?
The proof of the pudding is in the eating"
(Matt. 11:19, TM).

According to Robert Greenleaf, the best test—and one that is difficult to administer—for the servant leader is whether or not those who are served are growing.[1] Are they becoming healthier, wiser, freer, more autonomous? Are they more likely themselves to become servants?

There are six "core qualities" that flesh out the leadership-led relationship: trust, brokenness, gratefulness, hospitality, compassion, and endurance (see fig. 10-1). Remember, the leader's goal is to help the led. While exploring the rich relationship between the leader and the led, in the remaining chapters we will examine those qualities.

The first is trust.

Trust Is a Fundamental Quality

In the same way that trust in God is foundational to our beliefs as Christians, Christian servant leadership is rooted in a solid foundation of trust. Throughout the Bible, trust is highlighted as the characteristic building block of a relationship with God. Faith and trust are very closely related. We trust God. We trust His Word. "The just shall live by faith" (Gal.

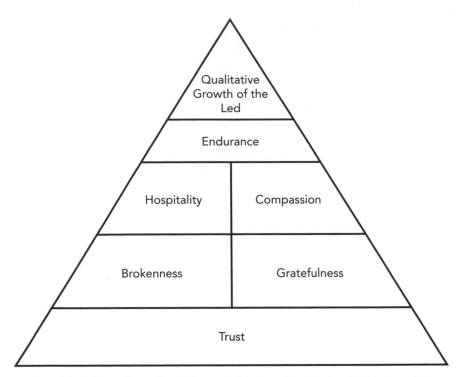

Fig. 10-1. The Core Qualities of the Leadership-Led Relationship

3:11, KJV). "By faith we accept God's grace" (see Eph. 2:8). "[Our] trust in the LORD [is] like Mount Zion, which cannot be shaken but endures forever" (Ps. 125:1).

As we know from past experience—from being both the leader and the led—unless those we lead trust *us*, our effectiveness to lead *them* is doubtful. The led will usually allow the leader time to build trust in their relationship; however, over time if trust cannot be established, the leader's effectiveness will decline. Trust has its DNA:

Trust Is a Two-Way Street

For the led to trust the leader, the leader must trust the led. In the words of Lovett H. Weems Jr., president of Saint Paul School of Theology in Kansas City, "People [follow] out of trust and that trust grows out of relationships and experience that engender such trust."

Trust Comes from a Common Language.

When church leaders begin reading supposedly secular books about leadership, it is often a great surprise that the language used in the best of books seems to come from the vocabulary of the church. Church leaders may expect to find elaborate grids, schemes, and designs. Instead, the words that dominate have to do with values and character. It soon becomes quite evident that there is no way to talk about leadership without talking about values, meaning, character, and relationships.

A term sometimes used in communication theory is the "ethical proof" of the speaker. "Ethical proof" refers to the credibility that the hearers accord the speaker. When the ethical proof is high, the task of persuading the audience is not hard. When the ethical proof is neutral, the speaker has a more difficult time. When the ethical proof is extremely negative, the speaker has a very difficult time persuading the audience. This concept means that the way the constituents perceive the leader is probably much more important than the "facts" of the presentation. So it is with the presence of trust and credibility between leaders and constituents.

James Kouzes speaks of credibility as "credit-ability." People are doing an analysis of our credibility all the time, just as a bank might assess our credit worthiness. Credibility is the working capital of the leader. It is the account of credibility that the leader draws from to make possible creative change. It's the foundation upon which all effective leadership builds.

Are you believable?

Are you dependable?

Are you trustworthy?

Do you act with integrity?

Do you foster feelings of security?

Psalm 15 is the creed of any leader who desires to lead *Christianly*. If its disciplined wisdom is applied with sincerity, it will reinvest dividends exponentially in your credibility account!

Trust Is Won Slowly and Lost Quickly

Once lost, trust is very difficult to regain in the leadership setting. People may give us a leadership position through election or employment. However, the credibility needed to lead must be earned among the people with whom we serve. It is trust from those with whom the leader works most closely that gives a leader the essential element of credibility.

Interaction with coworkers and family members is built on trust. Trust empowers us to be productive and efficient. When the level of trust is low, every interaction or exchange will have a "tax" imposed to make progress difficult. Efficiency grinds to a halt. Collaboration and collaborative change would not occur.

Leading in a "trust-vacuum" is impossible. So as Christian servant leaders, it is essential for us to encourage and develop trust. Borrowing from Weems, we discover three components that will help us to do this:

- Relationships
- Integrity
- Competence

RELATIONSHIPS

Relationships feed trust, and trust allows relationships to expand. Trust and relationships grow together. Expanding one requires expanding the other. Deepening relationships requires deepened trust. Relationships were a critical success factor to the apostle Paul's success in the early stages of Christianity. His experiences and writings show he built upon existing relationships to lead the church from afar. In Paul's letters we see how deeply he trusted the early Christians and how they must have trusted him.

For Christian servant leaders within their organizations, relationships precede plans and programs. Relationships are critical to successfully executed programs. Leaders may expect tacit acceptance of their leadership in the early stages of relationships; however, the relationship must grow for the group's outcomes to be achieved, for planned programs to succeed.

Lasting trust among those we lead comes from active, day-by-day interaction between the leader and the led, exploring and resolving active issues. That leader-led interaction requires the leader's presence. Thus, an active relationship is vital to build trust. The active presence and interaction between the leader and the led is communication. Paul traveled widely to visit personally with the growing church; then when unable to travel or when an issue needed to be addressed more quickly than he could arrange personally to be on-site, he wrote letters and sent emissaries.

Paul truly cared about those in the churches to whom he wrote. Likewise, our care of the led becomes vital for the led to continue investing in the relationship. Caring brings the relationship closer, and trust strengthens the relationship. Our success as leaders goes beyond just caring. It achieves the same degree of caring that Paul had for the early Christians; it reaches the level of love. Secular writers make the same point in saying "just possibly the best-kept secret of successful leaders is love."[2]

So relationships are how trust is developed, and as leaders, we need to be actively engaged, day-by-day, in those relationships. Furthermore, as in the case of Paul, we need to take our caring to the level of love for those we lead.

INTEGRITY

Integrity builds trust by having honesty and consistency be mandatory parts of the leader's words and deeds. Just as faith and works go hand in hand and work together, integrity and trust are complementary. Increased integrity builds trust; the lack of integrity erodes trust. Notice that integrity is not perfection. Rather, it is *consistency*. The leader's words and actions are consistent with each other; they work in concert.

In Ps. 25:21, David puts his integrity right alongside his righteousness as his dual protectors. Jesus spoke about integrity when He told the parable of the master and the dishonest manager. He also warned us that being honest with a little is just as important as being honest with a lot. Furthermore, He said that if we cannot be trusted with worldly wealth, how can we be trusted with the "true riches" of God's kingdom (Luke 16:1-12). So, as we have heard for many years, we build our own reputation, both with those we lead and with God. For those we lead, we must maintain the highest integrity, or consistency between word and deed.

This section is about the proof of effective leadership, which is the qualitative growth of the led. The format for leader-led interaction is relationships; relationships are where trust is built and integrity (or consistent words and actions) help the leader build the trust of the led. For the proof of successful servant leadership to occur, the consistent example and power of integrity are required.

COMPETENCE

Competence is another component of trust. Speaking plainly, our followers look to us to be able to accomplish what needs to be done. If we consistently fall short, trust will dissolve. The leader must effectively address the group's current needs.

So trust occurs in and from relationships, integrity (consistency between words and deeds) is vital to building trust, and competence (the ability to address the organization's needs) is necessary for building long-term trust. As leaders, we know that after an initial honeymoon period in any relationship, the led expect the leaders to meet expectations with competence to get the job done. In the religious arena, this expectation takes on additional weight. As Jackson W. Carroll points out in *Mainline to the Future*, a study of very large congregations found that their pastoral leaders "establish their authority or right to lead not primarily by virtue of the office they hold or because of their formal credentials, but more by *a combination of demonstrated competence and religious authenticity*" (emphasis added).[3] Thus, competence and integrity work together.

- *Competence Means Getting Things Moving*

Competence has everything to do with your MQ, your "Motion Quotient!" While others emphasize the need for a high IQ or EQ, it is imperative that we remember neither brilliance nor intelligence is synonymous with competence. *The sought-after skill is listening, analysis, and action to conclusion.* It is to hear, to understand, then to lead the group to appropriate action.

Whether or not we are aware, the led will hold us accountable to address the need. Our ability to successfully address the need is a reflection of our competence. Being competent is helping the group work through the task to successful conclusion. It is not the leader's ability to single-handedly accomplish the task, but rather the ability to understand the task and assure it is completed many times by the group. In a Christian institutional setting, the leader's competence is demonstrated by the ability to achieve objectives using a collaborative approach so the led accomplish the task.

- *Competence Is Listening and Focused Action*

Another aspect of competence is the ability to stay focused. If achieving the task collaboratively is desirable, then the leader's job is to keep the group focused on the task until successfully accomplished. Doing so is competence. This focus must be coupled with appropriate action and a working knowledge of the task at hand. Competence requires the leader to become familiar with the task at hand, even if the leader does not personally perform the work. Competence requires work on the part of the leader.

Trust Needs a Vision

To become leadership, trust needs another ingredient, vision or inspiration. Vision and inspiration propel the engine of trust to leadership. Otherwise, without vision or inspiration, the trusted person becomes a gatekeeper or a competent manager or administrator, not a leader.

Trust + Vision = Leadership

Putting the equation together . . .

VISION TRANSFORMS INANIMATE TRUST INTO A LIVING, EFFECTIVE LEADERSHIP

Trust alone does not make leadership, especially Christian leadership. The New Testament shows repeatedly how Jesus Christ continually portrayed vision passionately to inspire His followers. Reflecting back on a basic tenet, how does the life of Christ change how we carry out our roles as leaders? The answer is vision. Just as Christ's leadership coupled a strong vision with trust to be a strong leader, the successful Christian servant leader must also couple vision to trust. Without vision, the leader becomes a manager of the status quo. With vision and trust, the leader moves the led forward.

VISION WITH PASSION AND COMMITMENT INSPIRE THE PEOPLE BEING LED

Christ worked tirelessly at this. By His example, we see that being a leader requires vision and passion, and that they are conveyed by energy. Vision and inspiration require work. Vision with passion, commitment, and dedication inspires the led to achieve beyond what they anticipated.

The leader with trust and no vision administers or maintains the status quo. The leader with vision and no trust will have a short tenure as leader, since the leader needs the led. A leader abandoned by the led is no longer leading.

CHRIST'S VISION WAS RADICAL

As an inspirational leader with a vision, Jesus is an interesting example and role model for developing servant-leadership qualities and characteristics. Jesus passionately declared a singular vision to a heterogeneous community at the crossroads of the Mediterranean world. He departed philosophically from the conventional wisdom of the Jewish faith and its various groups, as well as the Roman culture. Yet with inspired vision that reached beyond the world known to His followers, He was able to be the ultimate servant and the ultimate leader.

Following the example of Jesus, the vision to transform trust into leadership need not be complex. Repeatedly, Jesus' disciples and apostles communicated a simple vision to the new church: Accept Jesus into your heart to be saved. In the case of our being the servant leader, our vision should be equally simple and straightforward. The vision should be short and very easy for anyone among the led to explain.

Vision brings trust alive. Vision is the propellant of trust. Likewise, trust is the harness of vision. Vision passionately pursued can exceed the bounds placed on it by trust, the trust earned from integrity and competence and developed in relationships. Vision can become its own master. We have all seen examples of this happening where the vision exceeds the bounds placed on it by the trust of the led. Jesus speaks directly to this risk in the

Beatitudes (Matt. 5:3-12), especially verse 5: "Blessed are the meek, for they will inherit the earth." No leader is exempt from the accountability of his flock. This is especially true for the servant leader. The leader's drive and vision must never exceed the trust placed on the leader by the led such that the trust is expendable in favor of achieving the vision.

PLAN...

11
BROKENNESS

"For You, O God, have tested us; You have refined us as silver is refined. You brought us into the net; You laid affliction on our backs. You have caused men to ride over our heads; we went through fire and through water; but You brought us out to rich fulfillment" (Ps. 66:10-12, NKJV).

Brokenness is the second core quality on which servant leadership is built. The relationship between brokenness and leadership in the real world of the Christian community often presents conflicting expectations and multiple demands for the leader. In these situations, how do you lead Christianly, consistently, and with vision and courage? Additionally, how can you lead when you feel abused, manipulated, undermined, or ignored? And why has God permitted painful words or deeds? What does He want to teach you? What does He want to teach others by your experience? What is the relationship between pastoral leadership and the brokenness of spirit you often experience in these situations?

Listen to the Covenant Prayer John Wesley often used at the beginning of each new year:

I am no longer my own, but Yours.
   Put me to what You will,
Rank me with whom You will.
   Put me to doing, put me to suffering.

115

Let me be employed by You or laid aside for You.

Exalted for You or brought low by You.

Let me have all things, let me have nothing.

I freely and heartily yield all things to Your pleasure and disposal.

And now, O glorious and blessed God,

Father, Son, and Holy Spirit,

You are mine, and I am Yours.

So be it.

And the covenant which I have made on earth,

Let it be ratified in heaven. Amen.[1]

Brokenness Exemplified

Notice Wesley's words:

"Suffering"

"laid aside for you"

"brought low by you"

"have nothing"

"disposal"

They are the expressions of surrender to circumstances—expressions of one who has braved the chilling winds, endured the hurtful taunts, borne the heavy cross, and yet courageously continued to pursue his or her mission and ministry. How could one lead so effectively as "a wounded healer," in the words of Nouwen? The present question: How can *you* lead "with a broken heart"? How can *any* servant leader hope for the desired results of qualitative change among the led with a heart that has been broken by circumstances? The answer is that it is a *proof* of leadership.

Brokenness Defined

Brokenness is one of those things that is easy to recognize when experienced but often difficult to describe. It could be said that brokenness is a sudden or expected hurt that weighs so heavily on the heart it takes your focus from your mission or ministry. Brokenness varies in degrees from uncomfortable to seemingly unbearable emotional pain. Sometimes God uses it when He needs to get your attention. Such was the case with Job and his trials.

Sometimes things happen that are outside of your control, as in the case of the apostle John's exile on the island of Patmos. God does not cause the circumstances (James 1:13); however, His sovereign purpose *allows* them to happen. God can use your brokenness to draw you closer to Him and to experience His healing. Psalm 51:17 says, "The sacrifices of God are a broken spirit, a broken and contrite heart—these, O God, You will not despise" (NKJV).

The Purpose of Brokenness

God uses brokenness in helping us develop character. Second Peter 1:5-9 says,

> For this very reason, make every effort to add to your faith goodness; and to goodness, knowledge; and to knowledge, self-control; and to self-control, perseverance; and to perseverance, godliness; and to godliness, brotherly kindness; and to brotherly kindness, love. For if you possess these qualities in increasing measure, they will keep you from being ineffective and unproductive in your knowledge of our Lord Jesus Christ. But if anyone does not have them, he is nearsighted and blind, and has forgotten that he has been cleansed from his past sins.

In the book *Broken in the Right Place: How God Tames the Soul*, Alan Nelson makes some powerful statements regarding brokenness:

"Brokenness purifies our ambitions."

"Brokenness allows us to see our own blind spots."

"The breaking process produces a leader that can be trusted."

He also quotes Paul Cho, "I've yet to see a leader God has used tremendously who has not been broken."[2]

Questions for Facing Brokenness

The following questions will help you assess your attitude for confronting brokenness:

- Are you willing to let go of your dreams and ambitions, if such is God's will?
- Are you defensive when accused, criticized, or misunderstood?
- Do you covet what others have instead of waiting for heaven's rewards?
- Do you forgive when offended, with or without an apology?
- Do you complain or argue out of rights that are unsurrendered?
- Do you think of others first, out of love?
- Do you proudly project that you are always right or know all the answers?
- Are you practicing the spiritual disciplines (prayer, fasting, solitude, simplicity, etc.)?
- Are you silent regarding self-promotion and letting God do your public relations?
- Do you daily say, "God, whatever it takes, I'm willing to submit to Your leadership?"
- Do you express joy in the difficulties that serve to refine you?
- Do you take risks out of obedience to Christ instead of giving into fear, pride, or denial?

The leader who allows himself or herself to go through the breaking process reverently, obediently, gracefully, and productively is a leader that is not only growing in character but also casting a wider net of influence.

The Fruits of Brokenness

No one actively seeks the pain, or sometimes even the shame, of brokenness. But when it happens, it can have a positive—and even fruitful—effect. The trimmed tree understands. The clipped rosebush gets it. The rain-drenched lily knows. All of nature is driven to beauty or strength by the breaking process. It's the same for God's highest creation. Brokenness can blossom in inner beauty. There is development in the valley as well as on the mountaintop.

In particular, what benefits are there to the Christian leader who victoriously walks the road of brokenness? The answer is simple: There is growth along the way. The fruits of brokenness are humility, authenticity, integrity, and sensitivity. All of these qualities are desirable as a leader. Pause and focus more closely on one of those "fruits of brokenness"—the fruit of humility.

"Humility" is another word that is difficult to define but necessary to experience if the leader is to be effective. Remember Eph. 4:1-2: "As a prisoner for the Lord, then, I urge you to live a life worthy of the calling you have received. Be completely humble and gentle; be patient, bearing with one another in love." Again in Prov. 15:33: "Before honor is humility" (NKJV).

In the Bible, humility is a prerequisite to the things leaders seek most in their vocation. Notice these seven ways—very common ways—to spot a humble spirit:

1. Humility does not demand its own way.
2. Humility exudes an attitude of service (service is doing mundane things that help others).
3. Humility does not seek attention or credit.
4. Humility forgives when offended but is hard to offend.
5. Humility does not criticize others.
6. Humility produces a teachable spirit.
7. Humility is gracious and thankful.

In fact, one of the most godly attributes you can express is a gracious spirit—a spirit of mercy and thanksgiving.

Romans 12:21 says, Humble servants "overcome evil with good." The paragraph heading in the *New International Version* for the great *kenosis* passage, Phil. 2:1-11, is "Imitating Christ's Humility." The passage reads:

> If you have any encouragement from being united with Christ, if any comfort from his love, if any fellowship with the Spirit, if any tenderness and compassion, then make my joy complete by being like-minded, having the same love, being one in spirit and purpose. Do nothing out of selfish ambition or vain conceit, but in humility consider others better than yourselves. Each of you should look not only to your own interests, but also to the interests of others.

Your attitude should be the same as that of Christ Jesus: Who, being in very nature God, did not consider equality with God something to be grasped, but made himself nothing, taking the very nature of a servant, being made in human likeness. And being found in appearance as a man, he humbled himself and became obedient to death—even death on a cross! Therefore God exalted him to the highest place and gave him the name that is above every name, that at the name of Jesus every knee should bow, in heaven and on earth and under the earth, and every tongue confess that Jesus Christ is Lord, to the glory of God the Father.

Responding to Brokenness

Leaders can respond in one of two ways to brokenness: (1) they can resent the situation, person, circumstance, or God, and grow bitter, become angry, and withdraw; or (2) they can be driven to their knees to ask God what He wants to teach them through this "dark night of the soul." They need to learn certain things about themselves if they are to grow and mature in their faith and in their calling during these times. In turn, this will enhance the core qualities of servant leaders and enhance their ability to achieve the goal of qualitative change among the led, which, again, is the proof of servant leadership.

God often uses "problem" people to teach servant leaders about themselves. As strong as leaders think they are, in the face of heartbreaking problems, they recognize their weakness and how much they need the Heavenly Father if they are to lead in the way He wants them to lead. Too often it seems that servant leaders are driven to their knees with the words of 2 Cor. 12:9: "But he said to me, 'My grace is sufficient for you, for my power is made perfect in weakness.'"

Servant leaders are to respond to brokenness
- By yielding responsibility of the "led" to the Christ who indwells them by His Spirit.
- By living in, through, and from the spiritual disciplines of prayer, Bible study, solitude, and so on.

- By living a "grace"-filled life (a theology of grace).
- By focusing on their walk and relationship with Christ and not on the expectations of others.
- By leading pastorally out of the pain and brokenness (not denying it).
- By acknowledging weaknesses and their total dependency upon the Christ who indwells with His Spirit. He is the One who will empower, guide, and comfort leaders who seek to lead out of their brokenness.
- By expecting trials, temptations, misunderstandings, verbal abuse, and rejection from those you are supposed to lead.
- By relating to those in the Christian fellowship who profess faith in Christ as brothers and sisters in Christ (even though evidence may not support their testimony).

The familiar prayer of Francis of Assisi embodies the *spirit* of the broken leader in Ps. 66. Pray it as you seek strength to lead in times of crisis, even as you are strengthening the faith of those whom you are leading:

Lord, make me an instrument of Thy peace;
Where there is hatred, let me sow love; Where there is injury, pardon;
Where there is doubt, faith; Where there is despair, hope;
Where there is darkness, light; Where there is sadness, joy.
O Divine Master, grant that I may not so much seek
—To be consoled as to console,
—To be understood as to understand,
—To be loved as to love;
For it is in giving that we receive;
It is in pardoning that we are pardoned;
It is in dying that we are born to eternal life.

PLAN . . .

12
GRATEFULNESS

"Whatever you do, whether in word or deed, do it all in the name of the Lord Jesus, giving thanks to God the Father through him"
(Col. 3:17).

Five thousand delegates from 192 countries participated in a 10-day conference. At the time of the conference the Berlin Wall stood firm. The Central and Eastern Europe Soviet bloc remained intact. Numerous African countries were involved in civil wars.

The highlight of the conference was the testimonies of God's grace from the delegates of those and other countries where Christians were regularly persecuted. These believers accepted 1 Thess. 5:18 as an imperative and a way of life for them: "Give thanks in all circumstances, for this is God's will for you in Christ Jesus."

Two weeks later, a missionary who attended the conference was elected president of a major Christian organization. The president-elect and his wife agonized over the decision to accept the position that was being offered. Among the reasons for their hesitation was the fear that they would forget the core values of the people they had served during their overseas appointment.

"They were such grateful people," the missionary said. "In spite of their substandard living conditions, they were so free to express gratitude to God for their numerous blessings."

The missionary couple hesitated to return to their home country. Cynicism and materialism were so pervasive there. Their "adopted" country exhibited few of those characteristics.

Sensing God's direction to accept the new ministry, they made the move. Years later they felt as if they had been sucked into the very lifestyle and mind-set that made them question their decision in the first place. During a chapel service held at the organization's headquarters, its president—the former missionary—heard a message delivered by guest speaker Brennan Manning.

His words struck a chord of response. Manning proposed a stirring question, "Let's say I interviewed ten people, asking each the question, 'Do you trust God?' and each answered, 'Yes, I trust God,' but nine of the ten actually did *not* trust Him. How would I find out which one of the professing Christians was telling the truth?" He continued, and offered the answer, "I would videotape each of the ten lives for a month. After watching the videos, I would pass judgment using this criterion: the person with an abiding spirit of gratitude is the one who trusts God."[1] God stamped the truth on the former missionary's heart. He would have to trust God in spite of his surroundings. He would have to set the standard of positive praise in the place where God stationed him. His own gratefulness would be the benchmark.

God desires a thankful people, not a murmuring, grumbling, faultfinding, and complaining people. Leading within the Christian community will not guarantee that you will avoid such attitudes. Even there, you will struggle to maintain an environment of gratitude.

No less real is God's power to equip your heart to be a grateful heart! Look again to 1 Thess. 5:18: "Give thanks in all circumstances, for this is God's will for you in Christ Jesus." It's the gold standard, the mark of discipleship and the mark of a vibrant Christian organization.

The text reminds us that our gratefulness must be *attentive* ("Give thanks"), *inclusive* ("in all circumstances"), and *God-centered* ("for this is God's will in Christ Jesus"). Let's look carefully at each one of these imperatives of gratitude, the third core quality upon which successful servant leadership is built. Each one is an essential characteristic of a consistently grateful Christian and therefore a characteristic of a more effective servant leader.

Our Gratefulness Must Be Attentive—*"Give thanks"* (v. 18a)

You recall the story of the ten lepers cleansed by Jesus (Luke 17:11-19). Ten were cleansed and sent on their way; yet only one returned to thank his healer. Were the other nine aware they had been cleaned? Of course! But they were seemingly more focused on the miracle than the Master who had performed it. Obviously, thanksgiving wasn't in their game plan.

But gratefulness should be in the game plan of every Christian leader—and every organization he or she may lead. Agreed, overflowing gratitude is not a "common" reaction to God's blessings. Some spiritual eye surgery may need to be performed. Attentiveness to what God is doing is best "seen" with our spiritual eyes.

With a closer attention, we may discover some overlooked blessings. We may find our equivalent to the crossing of the Red Sea, the pillar of fire by night and the manna by day, the daily protections from our enemies, or the healing of our own "leprosy." And with this new and more attentive look at God's moving in our lives, we are more than obligated to express our gratitude—gratitude to the One who promised never to leave us or forsake us.

Preoccupied with busyness, "the tyranny of the urgent," and the incessant running to and fro to the demands of others may cause us to lose spiritual focus, to overlook the work that God is doing in our lives, even as we're working in the lives of others.

A Spirit-empowered attentiveness to God will alert us to His presence. He may speak to us in unexpected ways—a song, the flight of a bird, the shine of the sun on a daffodil, a warm embrace, the encouraging word of a friend or family member, a newborn baby, a fresh blanket of snow, a full moon, a sunrise, a sunset, or a rainbow. The list of surprise reminders is as endless as the sands of the sea (which He also placed as a reminder of His power and presence).

And what about the grace-gifts from individuals—people with whom we live, work, or worship, colleagues within the organization we lead? Through attentiveness to God's activities in our lives, the people around us and the places we work can become a source of joy—abiding joy—even in the midst of seemingly impossible situations. Our gratefulness must be attentive.

Our Gratefulness Must Be Inclusive— "in all circumstances" (v. 18b)

Job asks, "If we take happiness from God's hand, must we not take sorrow too?" (see Job 2:10). Nouwen wrote about the spiritual work of gratitude: "To be grateful for all of our lives—the good as well as the bad, the moments of joy as well as the moments of sorrow, the successes as well as the failures, the rewards as well as the rejections—that requires hard spiritual work."

Don't focus just on the circumstances you normally would call "wonderful." God may use difficult circumstances in a wonderful way. So we thank Him in the difficult circumstances also! Manning told the story of a grateful, elderly woman in an extended care hospital:

> She had some kind of "wasting" disease, her powers fading away over the march of the month. A student worker spoke to her on a coincidental visit. The student kept going back, drawn by the strange force of a woman's joy. Though she could no longer move her arms and legs, the elderly lady would say, "I'm just so happy I can move my neck." When she could no longer move her neck, she would say, "I'm just so glad I can hear and see." When the young student finally asked the old woman what would happen if she lost sound and sight, the gentle old lady said, "I'll just be so grateful that you come to visit."[2]

Remember to be grateful for all things, including the little things. Jesus said, "Whosoever can be trusted with very little can also be trusted with much" (Luke 16:10). If you are grateful in small things, even in a small way, you will naturally express gratitude in greater things.

Thank You, God, even in these times, for the lessons You are teaching me about myself, my relationship to You, and others.

Our Gratefulness Must Be God-Centered— *"for this is God's will for you"* (v. 18c)

The theocentric, or God-centered, character of gratitude is anchored in ruthless trust that there is a God who is sovereign and whose providential care guides His people. By divine mercy, we have been given the unearned gift of salvation. We received this gift through no merit of our own. Our sins have been forgiven through the blood of Jesus Christ. And by divine mercy, we have received the promised Comforter, the Holy Spirit. We have been given a source of spiritual understanding and power that can help us rise above the tides of the times.

Celebrate the spiritual gifts you have received—gifts that can never be repaid! See if the tenor of your life doesn't become one of humble, joyful thanksgiving. Rejoice in the gifts and watch others take notice. "Give thanks to the LORD, for he is good; his love endures forever" (Ps. 107:1). "[Now] thanks be to God for his . . . gift [of grace]" (2 Cor. 9:15).

The testimony of one Christian worker exemplified this principle. She said, "I am learning new ways to see life and work as a means to express gratitude to God for His grace, mercy, and faithfulness." Learn some "new ways" to express your thanksgiving for God's eternal grace and mercy. Not only will it refresh your own heart, but the runoff will bless those you lead as well.

Our Gratefulness Focuses on God's Goodness Rather than People's Grumblings—*"in Christ Jesus"* (v. 18d)

The Christ-centered life is a life of constant thanksgiving—even in the face of ingratitude. Every spiritual blessing is given to us in our relationship with Christ. He is the Fountain of Grace, the Living Water, the Bread, and the Light. Unbelievably, some would even grumble about Jesus, debating

His genealogy, His birthday, and His promises. In the face of the debate, it should be noticed that the opposite of gratitude is ingratitude; and the antithesis of giving thanks is grumbling.

Grumbling has become the sport of choice among the citizens of our society. It's not a new problem, however. Ingratitude and negative attitudes were among the Israelites' major problems and caused them to wander in the wilderness for 40 years before entering the Promised Land. (And most of the time, they were grumbling while they were picking up manna from heaven!)

Grumblers are like the crew of vineyard workers in Jesus' parable who had labored from dawn to dusk and felt cheated when the latecomers received the same wage (Matt. 20:1-16). Grumblers bellyache about the unfairness of life, the poverty of their resources, the insensitivity of their spouse or employer, the liberals, the conservatives, the hot weather, the cold weather, the rich, the poor, the inadequate—whatever seems to be the "grumble special of the day." It is not *joy* that makes you grateful; it is *gratitude* that makes you joyful!

Too often we are not grateful because we are sad when things don't go our way. And they *won't always go our way*. Christ made one cross-generational, cross-situational promise to every Christian leader about leading grumblers: "I have told you these things, so that in me you may have peace. In this world you will have trouble. But take heart! I have overcome the world" (John 16:33).

As a Christian leader, a servant leader, gratefulness can become the basic attitude of your life. Let it be so! Give thanks to God in the midst of the most difficult situations. It is the oxygen of spiritual life that will support you during the breathtaking situations of leadership. Don't let the routines of life dull you to the surprises of God!

PLAN...

13
HOSPITALITY

"Offer hospitality to one another without grumbling"
(1 Pet. 4:9).

The fourth core quality of the servant leader, hospitality, has been a way of life fundamental to Christian identity for 1,700 years of the Christian Church. Christine Pohl convincingly documents this practice in her book *Making Room: Recovering Hospitality in Christian Tradition.*

Having wrestled with the biblical and historic understanding of hospitality in the Christian tradition—including its pain, limitations, and the leadership implications—we want to address the concept of "spiritual hospitality." It is at the heart of transformational relationships!

Biblically and theologically, the term "hospitality" is not limited to receiving a stranger into our homes—although it surely includes this dimension. It is rather an attitude toward others. Scriptural (spiritual) hospitality challenges us to relate to others *as if* we were relating to Christ himself.

The life and ministry of Jesus on earth serves as a textbook on hospitality. From His presence at the wedding at Cana, to the feeding of the five thousand, to the distribution of bread during the Last Supper, to serving breakfast on the beach following His resurrection, Jesus demonstrated the dynamics of His relationship to the disciples with hospitality. Some of His most important lessons were taught in the casual classrooms of Judea.

"Hospitality" means the "creation of free space"—making room, to use Pohl's words, where the strange and the stranger can enter and become friends. It is being to others a "living witness of the risen Christ." The gift of Christian hospitality is the opportunity we provide for the guest, stranger, or friend to find his or her own way, even in the context of differences of thought or behavior.

Making space for others affords them the opportunity to enter into deeper contact with themselves, with others, and with God. The result is often a healing relationship and the creation of a faith *community*. Hospitality offers the following:

friendship without bonds

unity without artificiality

freedom without abandonment

faith without demeaning

respect for individual differences

Having determined that spiritual hospitality is more than a meal and that it is a state of mind—or *state of the heart*—let's examine its important components.

Spiritual Hospitality Is a Love Gift *from* Christ

The miracle of miracles is that *we* are blessed when we reach out to others. Christ turns our "gifts of hospitality" *to others* into personal gifts *to us*. We find our Lord in the midst of our service to others. One of the most stirring acts in Scripture is the account of Jesus washing the feet of His disciples. It was both a spiritual and a practical act of kindness. Dusty from their journey along Judean highways, the customary foot washing would be an act of cleanliness. However, the "spiritual" act sprang from Christ's laying aside His heavenly authority to express His earthly humanity. John 13:1-5 says,

> It was just before the Passover Feast. Jesus knew that the time had come for him to leave this world and go to the Father. Having loved his own who were in the world, he now showed them the full extent of his love.

The evening meal was being served, and the devil had already prompted Judas Iscariot, son of Simon, to betray Jesus. Jesus knew that the Father had put all things under his power, and that he had come from God and was returning to God; so he got up from the meal, took off his outer clothing, and wrapped a towel around his waist. After that, he poured water into a basin and began to wash his disciples' feet, drying them with the towel that was wrapped around him.

The disciples would learn no greater lesson in expressing kindness to others. Jesus had given a love gift in the form of an act of humility and grace. How often we experience God's abiding presence in the midst of our own expressions of making room and creating space for those with whom we live and work.

The disciples also learned that Jesus' act of "spiritual hospitality" was meant to be shared in the lives of others. That is seen in the same Scripture passage (vv. 12-15):

When he had finished washing their feet, he put on his clothes and returned to his place. "Do you understand what I have done for you?" he asked them. "You call me 'Teacher' and 'Lord,' and rightly so, for that is what I am. Now that I, your Lord and Teacher, have washed your feet, you also should wash one another's feet. I have set you an example that you should do as I have done for you."

Nouwen would define compassionate actions or spiritual hospitality as "being to *others* what Saint John was for his listeners and readers: A living *witness* of the risen Christ!" Something happens *to us* and *through us* as we reach out to others with gifts of hospitality. A qualitative change occurs in the servant leader as well as in the led. The grace of Christ flows to us and through us when we work, play, and study with the mind of Christ!

Our tendency, however, is to hesitate because we feel our "gifts" are so insignificant. Brennan Manning told an applicable story titled "The Cracked Pot." In this tale a water bearer daily carries two pots of water from a stream to his master's house. One pot is cracked and the other is whole. The cracked water pot always loses half its water on the journey to the house. One day the cracked pot apologizes to the water bearer for losing water. The water bearer comforts the water pot by showing it that along the side of the path on which it is carried beautiful flowers are growing. The water bearer explains that he planted flower seeds along that side of the path, knowing that the water pot would water the seeds through its crack. The bearer adds that he picks these flowers regularly to beautify his master's house and that this would not be possible if the water pot were anything other than what it is.[1]

In our efforts at spiritual hospitality, do we sometimes feel like the "cracked pot"? Of course! But God uses our availability and our efforts in ways we could never imagine. And in the process, He blesses us in ways we never dreamed possible! Miraculously, *we* are blessed when we express spiritual hospitality to others.

Spiritual Hospitality Is a Love Gift *to* Christ

Colossians 3:23-24 reminds us that our service to others is service to the Lord Christ: "Whatever you do, work at it with all your heart, as working for the Lord, not for men, since you know that you will receive an inheritance from the Lord as a reward. It is the Lord Christ you are serving." This concept is at the very core of servant leadership. In our efforts we can be hurt, misunderstood, and rejected; or we can be appreciated, affirmed, and accepted. The response, however, does not dictate our action. We love because He first loved us.

A ministry professional and his wife moved to a country in Southeast Asia. Both were overwhelmed by the pervasiveness of poverty there. The wife shared her despair with a friend, a resident of the country. The friend encouraged her to focus on the few she could help, not on the masses she could not. The wife took her advice and focused on some women in need. She bought glasses for one lady, new teeth for another, and for another she sponsored a beautician's course and attended the graduation ceremony. She befriended these ladies and often invited them to her home. By serving those few, she was serving Christ—and exemplifying Matt. 25:40: "The King will reply, 'I tell you the truth, whatever you did for one of the least of these brothers of mine, you did for me.'"

Our gifts of hospitality to others are not selective "spiritual gifts" given by God to only a few for use in the Kingdom. Rather, they are practical expressions of our love for Christ. Granted, this commitment to a lifestyle of "spiritual hospitality" brings key action questions to mind:

- What can I do to be hospitable in my servant leadership? Where can I be hospitable?
- How will my attitude of hospitality impact the way I live, learn, and lead?
- How do I deal with my unfinished agenda for the day when I attempt to "create space" and make room for others and in so doing not accomplish what I think needs to get done?

These are real-life questions with which we must grapple. Spiritual hospitality takes time, patience, and understanding.

Henri Nouwen begins an article on compassion with an old Sufi story of a "watermelon hunter."

> Once upon a time, there was a man who strayed from his own country into the world known as the Land of Fools. He soon saw a number of people fleeing in terror from a field where they had been trying to reap wheat. "There is a monster in that field," they told him. He looked and saw that it was a watermelon.
>
> He offered to kill the "monster" for them. When he had cut the melon from its stalk, he took a slice and began to eat it. To his amazement, the people became even more terrified of him than they had been of the melon. They drove him away with pitchforks crying, "He will kill us next, unless we get rid of him."
>
> It so happened that at another time another man also strayed into the Land of Fools, and the same thing started to happen to him. But, instead of offering to help them with the "monster," he agreed with them that it must be dangerous and by tiptoeing away from it with them he gained their confidence. He spent a long time with them in their houses until he could teach them, little by little, the basic facts which would enable them not only to lose their fear of melons, but even to cultivate them themselves.[2]

With which "hunter" do you most identify? The second hunter was the servant leader. By solidarity with the led, trying to understand their concerns and spending quality time with them, the second "hunter" made a profound difference in the lives of the people in the story. He made a qualitative change in the lives of the led. His proof of leadership success was how they dramatically changed their perspective on melons. He "made room" and "created space" for these people who were different from him.

Spiritual Hospitality Is a *Way of Life*

Spiritual hospitality isn't defined by a single act of mercy. It is characterized by a lifestyle—acts or attitudes of kindness and compassion, fleshing out the principles of God's eternal Word in earthly endeavors. Creating space and making room for the strangers, the disenfranchised and lonely, our family members and friends. In one sense it is a perpetual journey on the scriptural "Jericho Road":

On one occasion an expert in the law stood up to test Jesus. "Teacher," he asked, "what must I do to inherit eternal life?"

"What is written in the Law?" he replied. "How do you read it?"

He answered: "Love the Lord your God with all your heart and with all your soul and with all your strength and with all your mind"; and, "Love your neighbor as yourself."

"You have answered correctly," Jesus replied. "Do this and you will live."

But he wanted to justify himself, so he asked Jesus, "And who is my neighbor?"

In reply Jesus said: "A man was going down from Jerusalem to Jericho, when he fell into the hands of robbers. They stripped him of his clothes, beat him and went away, leaving him half dead. A priest happened to be going down the same road, and when he saw the man, he passed by on the other side. So too, a Levite, when he came to the place and saw him, passed by on the other side. But a Samaritan, as he traveled, came where the man was; and when he saw him, he took pity on him. He went to him and bandaged his wounds, pouring on oil and wine. Then he put the man on his own donkey, took him to an inn and took care of him. The next day he took out two silver coins and gave them to the innkeeper. "Look after him," he said, "and when I return, I will reimburse you for any extra expense you may have."

"Which of these three do you think was a neighbor to the man who fell into the hands of robbers?"

The expert in the law replied, "The one who had mercy on him." Jesus told him, "Go and do likewise" *(Luke 10:25-37)*.

PLAN● ● ●

14
COMPASSION

"Therefore, as God's chosen people, holy and dearly loved, clothe yourselves with compassion, kindness, humility, gentleness and patience" (Col. 3:12).

The fifth core quality of the servant leader is the caring quality: compassion. Heartless leadership is probably as dangerous as *mindless* leadership. It certainly isn't Christlike. "When he saw the crowds, he had compassion on them, because they were harassed and helpless, like sheep without a shepherd" (Matt. 9:36). Leadership mission, vision, or objectives without a Christlike (and Christ-filled), compassionate heart is not relevant to true Christianity. In fact, it is contrary to the Word of God: "Finally, all of you, live in harmony with one another; be sympathetic, love as brothers, be compassionate and humble" (1 Pet. 3:8).

Compassion Is Caring

Compassion is nearly synonymous with *caring* in the life and leadership qualities of the servant leader. Our care for others can be direct or indirect. The word "care" finds its root in the Celtic term "kara," which means lament. So the basic meaning of care is "to grieve, to experience sorrow, to cry out with." The origin of the word is striking because we tend to look primarily at the caring of the strong toward the weak; or the powerful toward the powerless; or "haves" toward the "have-nots." Actually the word suggests inclusiveness. The spectrum is as wide or tall or deep as the Savior's love for humankind. It is one of the character traits that the apostle Paul envisioned for the Christians at Rome: "Rejoice with those who rejoice; mourn with those who mourn" (Rom. 12:15).

Compassion Is Enabling

Biblical compassion is not just a skill we acquire. Rather, it is a quality of the human heart that must be revealed or released—based upon our godliness and holiness. Psalm 103:13 says, "As a father has compassion on his children, so the LORD has compassion on those who fear him." The late Henri Nouwen often stated that you cannot get a Ph.D. in caring. It comes from a godly heart and is practiced in the "leadership trenches." He helps us realize that when we, as leaders, see others and discover in them gentleness, tenderness, and other beautiful gifts they are not able to see themselves, then our compassionate heart is revealed. What a profound thought! A compassionate heart enables others to see what they cannot see in themselves!

Again, we see the reciprocal part of servant leadership. As Christian servant leaders, we become conduits of God's caring or compassion—His hands and feet, His eyes and ears, His arms and shoulders. The *proof* of our leadership is in the enabling of others to see what they have not seen of their own worth or ability. To be compassionate is not something we do for others, but rather it is discovering with others their divinely given resources and inner qualities, and standing alongside them in their times of need. Compassion is not proving our validity to others; it is affirming their validity.

Compassion Is Exemplified

When we honestly ask ourselves which persons in our lives mean the most to us, it is usually those who—instead of giving much advice—have, rather, chosen to share our pain and touch our wounds with a gentle and tender hand. It is those who model the gentle shepherd in Jesus' parable of reaching to the lost sheep and lifting it to his shoulders—without recrimination.

The friend who can be silent with us in a moment of despair or confusion, who can stay with us in an hour of grief and bereavement, and who can tolerate our situation without knowing all the details is the friend who truly cares.

You may remember moments in which you were called to be with someone who had lost a friend or a family member. What did you say or do at such a moment? The first inclination was probably to offer words—to say things such as,

"Don't be sad. Your loved one is in the hands of God."

"You have so much to live for."

"God let this happen because you are so strong."

"You'll get through this and be much the better for it."

But compassion/caring often is being "seen and not heard." Being truly present, even in the quietness, and praying inwardly, honestly, and confidently for that person in need!

Nouwen introduces us to the phenomenal concept of "voluntary displacement" in his book titled *Compassion*[1] and in other books and numerous articles on the subject. Voluntary displacement means that for the sake of others, we willingly go to places we'd rather not go. We move out of our comfort zones voluntarily and "displace" ourselves outside the familiar to us. Why? A need exists; a response from within is required; an inward call from God is felt; we go, because of who we are. Voluntary displacement can take us to the inner city or around the world. This calling can be for a brief time or for a lifetime.

Nouwen's life illustrates how caring deeply for others often interrupts our routines of life. It really was not difficult for him to leave his teaching positions at Notre Dame, Harvard, and Yale divinity schools to accept an invitation to spend the final 10 years of his life living and working as priest to the L'Arche Community for the severely mentally handicapped in Toronto.

Compassion Is Contagious

Compassion reproduces its own kind. Especially in Christian leadership, one who motivates others with a gentle and understanding spirit will usually produce "followers" who will manifest the same spirit. New Testament church leaders learned to lead with a fatherly spirit by imitating their mentor, Paul:

> Even though you have ten thousand guardians in Christ, you do not have many fathers, for in Christ Jesus I became your father through the gospel. Therefore I urge you to imitate me. For this reason I am sending to you Timothy, my son whom I love, who is faithful in the Lord. He will remind you of my way of life in Christ Jesus, which agrees with what I teach everywhere in every church (*1 Cor. 4:15-17*).

Conversely, leadership by "bullying" produces additional bullies. And leadership by bullying is a proven way to shatter the very foundations of an organization—Christian or otherwise. Bullies are more interested in their own agenda, more interested in meeting their own needs than in meeting the needs of others. Bullies don't have a heart for their prey. They don't stop to listen or learn about the "other side of the story." They barge in, take over, and "take no prisoners." Their journey is always along a one-way street!

The bully mind is not the mind of Christ. In the midst of the "Calvary crisis," the Master could have forced His will. It was obvious in one awesome question: "Do you think I cannot call on my Father, and he will at once put at my disposal more than twelve legions of angels?" (Matt. 26:53). He chose rather to submit to others, because He was submitting to His Father's will, to open His heart to the hurts of those who falsely accused Him. Consequently, some of those same accusers became His faithful followers.

Compassion Is Proactive

It can be said not only that "Jesus saves" but also that "Jesus cares." During His earthly ministry, He was proactive in showing deeds of compassion to those who followed Him. "God anointed Jesus of Nazareth with the Holy Ghost and with power: who went about doing good, and healing all that were oppressed of the devil; for God was with him" (Acts 10:38, KJV). Someone once said that if Jesus "went about doing good," we can't settle for just going about! Our leadership ministry has a goal: healing and helping others.

The apostle Peter understood. Failing under the scrutiny of accusers during the trial of Jesus, Peter fearfully denied his Lord and suffered agonizing guilt. Jesus went to him and forgave him and loved him and restored him to ministry.

Servant leaders can take similar actions. Christlike compassion is always looking for ways to heal the hurts of others—including restoring them in spirit. Like Barnabas, they seek to be on the positive side of a problem, patiently training, not willing to be judgmental, helping others to discover their gifts, and opening doors of opportunity for them.

Barnabas was the one who took Saul (Paul) into the "fold" of discipleship. Later Paul would reflect the "Encourager" (Barnabas) in his own writings.

> Love is patient, love is kind. It does not envy, it does not boast, it is not proud. It is not rude, it is not self-seeking, it is not easily angered, it keeps no record of wrongs. Love does not delight in evil but rejoices with the truth. It always protects, always trusts, always hopes, always perseveres (*1 Cor. 13:4-7*).

Compassion Is Reactive

Compassion "listens before it leaps." It is willing to look deep into the heart of another, to understand that more is *unsaid* than is being said. So many of those we lead come from dysfunctional homes. They often utter words that were part of their family's vocabulary—hurtful, careless, or demeaning words. Compassion reacts in a way that understands diverse backgrounds.

Servant leaders look for the "Why?" behind the "What!" They ask the right questions (without prying or forcing answers). They express their own vulnerabilities. They are humble about their own forgiven past and are willing to forgive others of theirs. Their attitude is like that of Jesus who forgave the thief on the cross. He understood his curses, and He understood his con-

triteness. Christ's compassion made a place in paradise for one who had only moments before added to the misery of His final minutes on earth.

Compassion Is Cautious

The compassionate servant leader should seek the guidance of the
Holy Spirit at all times—especially in the midst of a compassion/caring situation. *Compassion* may be misunderstood as *affection*. Opening your
heart to "opened hearts" (vulnerable hearts) can lead to open-minded behavior, careless behavior. Caring deeply for someone in the time of need—
especially for someone of a different gender—can lead to a breakdown in
personal responsibility. Many lives and ministries have been shattered in
the "counselor's office." Counsel without caution has often led to emotional confusion. And emotional confusion has often led to physical attraction,
which then led to sinful actions.

Cautious compassion is alert to the work of the enemy. Remember
what 1 Pet. 5:8 says: "Be self-controlled and alert. Your enemy the devil
prowls around like a roaring lion looking for someone to devour." Cautious
compassion doesn't put itself in unwise situations. It always errs on the side
of precaution. It avoids the very appearance of wrong and yet seeks the wisdom of the Word and the promptings of the Holy Spirit to listen, care, and
stand alongside someone in his or her time of need.

The servant leader has a wonderful opportunity—and an awesome responsibility—to reflect the ministry of Christ in equipping others for their
own leadership. The core quality of compassion is a model for such a ministry.

PLAN• • •

15
ENDURANCE

*"Keep your head in all situations, endure hardship,
do the work of an evangelist, discharge all the duties
of your ministry"* (2 Tim. 4:5).

A military chaplain wrote to her Christian university professor, thanking him for his example and his instruction. She also said, "I'll never forget the class discussion about Paul's admonition to Archippus in Col. 4:17, "Do not walk away from the assignment God has given you" (author's paraphrase). She continued, "The most difficult assignment I have ever been given is to stay put and continue the work God gave me to do." She concluded, "Staying orders were a lot harder to obey than marching orders."[1]

Paul's message is the sixth and final core quality of the servant leader. The principle is clear: "Stay put, and keep working!" It was a message of endurance—one we might call an old-fashioned *stick-to-it-iveness*.

Endurance has always been an attribute vital to the Christian—and to the Christian leader. For example, on various occasions God commanded Moses to "Stay put!" Exodus 24:12 tells us of one occasion: "The LORD said to Moses, 'Come up to me on the mountain and stay here, and I will give you the tablets of stone, with the law and commands I have written for their instruction.'"

Isaiah the prophet underscored the rewards of such patient endurance:

"Those who wait for the LORD will gain new strength; they will mount up with wings like eagles, they will run and not get tired, they will walk and not become weary" (Isa. 40:31, NASB). Like a track coach giving a team some last-minute instructions before a track meet, the writer to the Hebrews echoed the advice of the prophet—adding the example of Christ: "Let us run with endurance the race that is set before us, fixing our eyes on Jesus, the author and perfector of faith, who for the joy set before Him endured the cross" (Heb. 12:1-2, NASB).

This endurance and clarity of purpose have also been the highlights of secular leadership. As prime minister of Great Britain during his country's most trying period, Sir Winston Churchill was asked to return to his high school to deliver an important speech. After a long and glowing introduction, Churchill arose, went to the podium, and gave one of the most memorable speeches in history: "Never, never, never, never give up!" Then he sat down. With just six words, the prime minister had captured the admonition of the apostle Paul to Archippus, "Do not walk away from the assignment God has given you." It's still some of the best advice available.

Probably every Christian leader has had that moment when he or she was ready to throw in the towel—to surrender to the situation, to *give up*. The core quality of endurance is necessary to overcome the temptation.

Notice several important things about endurance:

First, Notice the *Need* for Endurance

The Scriptures remind us of our human frailties in the face of our human responsibilities: "We have this treasure in jars of clay to show that this all-surpassing power is from God and not from us" (2 Cor. 4:7). God inspired and empowered tenacity—spiritual endurance—is as vital to a Christian leader as oxygen. We are humanly frail, but we have a heavenly work to do—in an earthly environment. We need some heavenly help! And God has promised just that. He doesn't *assign us* without promising to *empower us*. That was evident even *before* the day of Pentecost. Acts 1:8 says, "You will receive power when the Holy Spirit comes on you; and you will be my witnesses in Jerusalem, and in all Judea and Samaria, and to the ends of the earth."

We don't know why Paul was compelled to speak his words about not quitting to Archippus. We can only imagine what kind of circumstances would cause the New Testament leader's knees to shake, or tempt him to lay down the sword. But we do know they could have been similar to those we have faced! Like us, Archippus probably worked with some stubborn subordinates, faced financial pressures, felt the stalking shadows of the enemy, and experienced stress. He led people—just as we lead people. It's enough to make anyone's knees shake! But we don't have to lay down the sword.

Before we can formulate our personal plan for "staying put," we should examine some factors that enter our thoughts when we consider "walking away." There are common reasons why we're tempted to quit—to *give up* on a project, an assignment, a responsibility, or a calling before genuine release comes from the Lord.

Enemy Attacks

For sure, the enemy of our soul—and our ministry wants us to quit! He is constantly wrestling us over our calling: "Our struggle is not against flesh and blood, but against the rulers, against the authorities, against the powers of the dark world and against the spiritual forces of evil in the heavenly realms" (Eph. 6:12). According to the Bible, Satan's objectives are clearly stated. He aims to "kill," "steal," and "destroy" (see John 10:10). His stealth attacks on our mind come unannounced—but often after either a "high day" or a "low moment."

Difficult Problems

Another reason we're tempted to give up is the enormous difficulty of a certain situation. Some problems seem unsolvable. Moses must have felt that when he announced to Israel, "How can I bear your problems and your burdens and your disputes all by myself?" (Deut. 1:12). It is during those problem-solving times that we not only wish we had the leadership abilities of Moses but also cry out for the wisdom skills of Daniel. "This man Daniel, whom the king called Belteshazzar, was found to have a keen mind and knowledge and understanding, and also the ability to interpret dreams, explain riddles and solve difficult problems" (Dan. 5:12).

In their book *Mastering Ministry* Anne and Ray Ortlund talk about three periods (zones) all problems have in common:[2]

- **Zone A** is called "Desire to Achieve" and is characterized by idealism, naïveté, or apprehension.
- **Zone B** is called the "Desire to Quit" and is characterized by confusion and conflict, when problems arise. This is the danger zone: problems need to be identified, separated, spelled out, and tackled, one by one. Zone B will end in one of two ways: we will quit and abort the project, or we will endure with "bulldog" tenacity — resisting the temptation to quit. We can choose to believe that, even in a seemingly impossible situation, the God who has promised never to leave us or forsake us is present. We can choose to believe that, by the grace of God, there is a way through, over, under, or around the confusing situation.
- **Zone C** is called "Achievement and Growth." Christian leaders and the led characterize this zone by faith and personal satisfaction, and a sense of realism, maturity, and expectation.

Ministry Misconceptions

We are also tempted to quit because of misconceptions about the Christian life and Christian ministry:

"Progress is only being made when things are running smoothly."
"Bigger is better."
"Suffering and hardship can't be of God."
"Success is gaining everyone's approval."
"If you have enough faith, everything will just fall into place."

Misconceptions can happen over a longer period of ministry time; or they may happen the first week! Our professors or instructors have painted a Thomas Kincaid-like picture puzzle of our calling. Chapel speakers talked about their life-changing impact on the lives of others. We idealized our leadership role. But soon the pictured puzzle pieces separate in the winds of our work. We're left with a jumbled mess!

The problem is, we didn't hear about the *problems*! We didn't hear the "rest of the story." Too soon we discover that "friend days" are fewer than *workdays*. (And the workdays are often the loneliest days!) The reality of trying to form "perfect" plans is attacked by the realization that we are depending on imperfect people (including ourselves) to carry them out.

Physical and Emotional Limitations

Often our mind and body simply shut down. We've burned the candles at both ends. We've forsaken diet and exercise in favor of constant work. We've failed to gather an accountability partner (or team). We've ignored the warning signs and forged on. Physical and emotional limitations are simply part of being human. As we've noticed, Jesus called a timeout for His disciples. Paul took a few days off in Athens. Timothy was obviously involved in an exercise program. And Dorcas had a sewing circle.

Often, we blame the spiritual for our quitting (and sometimes rightly so), when the problem was actually a physical or emotional *sprain*. We might be better off to simply take a *rest* rather than a *run-for-it*!

Staff Limitations

Let's face it; all of our staff appointments aren't for the better. We may think so at the time. We may even feel that we have God's direction. But appointing staff means appointing people who have personal limitations—as well as underlying spiritual issues. Again using Paul as an example, he made staff appointments that didn't turn out as expected. The loneliness of leadership was clearly evident: "Do your best to come to me quickly, for Demas, because he loved this world, has deserted me and has gone to Thessalonica. Crescens has gone to Galatia, and Titus to Dalmatia. Only Luke is with me" (2 Tim. 4:9-11). Probably at some time in the process of the farewell dinners, the great New Testament leader momentarily felt like the military chaplain described at the beginning of the chapter, "Staying orders are a lot harder than marching orders."

But Paul endured. His mission was bigger than the mess he was in. Had he joined the exodus, the Church would not be in such an exciting position to offer hope to a hurting world. As well, other Christian leaders would not have the courage to "stay put" when the going gets rough.

Second, Notice the *Pain* of Endurance

It is often painful to "stay put" in the midst of conflict, misunderstanding, or power struggles. Vision, purpose, and motivation are on the bubble, while emotions take the heat. The tendency is to "move on" when the pressure builds, when you don't get your way, or when the recognition you receive doesn't meet your expectations.

"Enduring" through extraordinary times requires, *first*, a resolute faith in the God who has placed us in that situation. His grace, His presence, and His peace can calm our inner storms—and keep us on track. *Second*, it takes an inner resolve to wait for God's release. Time has proven the error of making a quick exit. Often, personal and organizational victories are just around the curve in the road. *Third*, in times of crisis we need to focus on whom we serve. Ultimately we answer to the One who appointed us: God. Boards or committees or people are merely used by Him to accomplish His purpose.

We can learn much about the pain of endurance from Ernest Shackleton and his 1914 Antarctic Expedition. Not known as a Christian leader, yet he taught us much about the necessity of endurance.

In August 1914, Ernest Shackleton, an intrepid British explorer, boarded the ship *Endurance*. He and his team of 27 men set sail for the South Atlantic. The group wanted to be the first to cross the continent of Antarctica.

Early the next year, their ship was trapped in the ice. By October 1915, still half a continent away from their intended base, the ship was crushed by ice and sank to the bottom of the ocean. In the months that followed, the crew's food and water disappeared. Shackleton and his men, drifting on ice packs, were castaways in one of the most savage regions of the world. Under Shackleton's leadership, they trekked over barren, frozen ice.

More than a year after the shipwreck Shackleton and his crew were stranded on an island at the tip of Antarctica. Their food was dwindling, and there appeared little hope of rescue. Survival, Shackleton realized, depended on a bold act. Leaving most of the crew behind and with only a few of his men, he knew he must reach a whaling outpost by crossing 800 miles of stormy seas in an open boat. Upon landing at St. George's Island, his only route to secure rescue for himself and his shipmates was still across an ominous range of glaciers and mountains that had never been crossed before. He took the chance. He had to endure. He and two others successfully reached the settlement. Amazingly, he saved his entire crew. Everyone survived. Everyone![3]

Paul's journeys, as outlined in the Book of Acts, were filled with similar experiences! Read Acts 27:25 again for Paul's advice to those struggling to survive a shipwreck: "Keep up your courage, men, for I have faith in God that it will happen just as he told me." Paul was sailing his own ship "Endurance":

- After being in jail for two years, Paul and others were on their way to Rome.
- Paul's admonition to the men onboard the ship was spoken in the middle of a typhoon, a shipwreck, and no food for 14 days (see vv. 13-44).
- *But,* God had earlier told Paul that he would "testify [of God's grace] in Rome" (Acts 23:11).

As painful as his situation was, Paul was convinced that God had everything under control. He was on a heavenly mission that Satan sidetracked in the form of a shipwreck. His answer: "I have faith in God."

Third, Notice the *Plan* for Endurance

The examples of others prove that servant leaders can endure even under the most difficult situations. Paul and Earnest Shackleton show that leading through extraordinary times and situations requires plans for enduring. The following strategies are taken from *Leading at the Edge: Leading Lessons from the Extraordinary Saga of Shackleton's Antarctic Expedition.*

- **Vision and Quick Victories:** Never lose sight of the ultimate goal and focus energy on short-term objectives.
- **Symbolism and Personal Example:** Set a personal example with visible, memorable symbols and behaviors.
- **Optimism and Reality:** Instill optimism and self-confidence but stay grounded in reality.
- **Stamina:** Take care of yourself: Maintain your stamina and let go of guilt.
- **The Team Message:** Reinforce the team message constantly: "We are one—we live or die together."
- **Core Team Values:** Minimize status differences and insist on courtesy and mutual respect.
- **Conflict:** Master conflict—deal with anger in small doses, engage dissidents, and avoid needless power struggles.
- **Lighten Up!** Find something to celebrate and something to laugh about.
- **Risk:** Be willing to take the Big Risk.
- **Tenacious Creativity:** Never give up—there's always another move.[4]

Fourth, Notice the *Gift* of Endurance

God's grace-gifts to the servant leader are seen in the book *Lead to Succeed: New Testament Principles for Visionary Leadership:*

> Some of the greatest spiritual miracles are birthed during the greatest earthly adversities. Needs are miraculously supplied. Hearts are miraculously tendered. Enemies are miraculously reconciled. Leadership miraculously surfaces. Jesus is still the master of the raging seas![5]

"Stick-to-it-iveness"—endurance or perseverance—is not a gift we give to other people. By no means! Rather, it is a grace-gift from God to *us* for the spiritual growth, Christian maturity, and personal development *we* experience. In exercising tenacity—staying power—we are the blessed.

In choosing to believe that God is in the midst of a process or problem, we may grow spiritually. We may mature in Christ significantly. Why? Because our help must come from God. We discover that our best leadership comes when we are on our knees—in dependency upon the One who has called us to our assignment, the One who will complete in us and our work exactly what He has designed!

On the quality of endurance, God spoke directly to Moses when he asked God to name someone else to be leader of the Jews in Egypt. God's reply to Moses was, "I am sending you to the King of Egypt so that you can lead my people out of Egypt." Moses said, "I am nobody. No, Lord, don't send me! I am a poor speaker, slow and hesitant. No, Lord, please send someone else." God responded to Moses: "I will be with you" (see Exod. 3:10-12).

God then gave Moses his credentials: "Tell them 'I AM' has sent you" (see v. 14). He is telling us the very same thing. The "I AM," who calls, empowers, keeps, and carries us not only sends us to our place of service but also supports us once we get there—and stay there!

Endurance, with Contentment!
What a Profound Gift from God to Us!

God's own gift of endurance allows us to respond with endurance. *His* endurance enables us to "stay the course" until He releases us from an assignment! And who benefits the most? Only God knows. But, for sure, we who "endure" by God's grace are blessed. Tenacity is a grace-gift from God to us!

"Do not walk away from the assignment God gives to you!"

POSTSCRIPT

Christian Hope for the Servant Leader

Napoleon Bonaparte is reported to have said, "Leaders are dealers in hope." For the Christian leader, this is especially true in situations within a faith community when good and godly people have clear and distinct differences over vision and values.

Months before the 2001-2 school year began, a school administrator was scheduled to speak on September 12, 2001, to students in a chapel service. The events of September 11 shook the campus to the core, as they did many around the world. The administrator prayed with students, staff, faculty, and their families as they came to the chapel/auditorium throughout the afternoon of September 11. At 6 P.M., the chaplain and his staff led the campus community in a meaningful service of prayer and reflection.

The administrator's sermon theme for the next morning's chapel service changed radically. With much prayer and not much sleep, he spoke to the campus family on the subject "Why Do Good People Suffer?" The text for the sermon was the Old Testament Book of Habakkuk. The entire campus, it seemed, was asking questions and seeking answers about the problem of evil and human suffering.

Habakkuk, you may remember, was an Old Testament prophet who was deeply distressed by the apparent injustice that prevailed in the world. He attempted to reconcile the evil of his day with the goodness and the righteous character of God.

As a prophet of God, he was concerned with the suffering of his people.

When God told Habakkuk that Babylon would conquer Israel, the prophet felt this was not just. Without hesitation, he asked God why He would allow a heathen and cruel nation—the Babylonians—to oppress *His* people. Why would He use such a nation to chastise them?

Following his complaints to God (see chapter 1), Habakkuk breaks forth in his search for answers with this startling affirmation: "The *just* shall *live* by his *faith*" (2:4, NKJV, emphasis added).

Habakkuk concludes his power-packed, three-chapter book with these words near the close of chapter 3:

> Though the fig tree does not bud and there are no grapes on the vines,
>
> though the olive crop fails and the fields produce no food,
>
> though there are no sheep in the pen and no cattle in the stalls,
>
> *yet*, I will rejoice in the LORD, I will be joyful in God my Savior (*vv. 17-18, emphasis added*).

The administrator's translation of these verses was as follows:

> When God appears silent, when there is no apparent evidence that God heard or even understood the situation, when all that I've worked for seems lost. In these moments, we choose to believe radically in a God who is faithful and true; we stake our lives on His promise to never leave us nor forsake us; and we pray, "We don't know what to do, but we are looking to you."

The faith of servant leaders, indeed all Christians, in these moments is not based on *feelings* but on the *conviction* that God is sovereign and will bring good out of every situation in which they find themselves. God dealt with Habakkuk patiently until he could see that Babylon was being used by God to discipline Israel and that Babylon itself would also face the judgment of God.

The providence of God does not mean that disappointment and trouble will not come. It does mean that *nothing, not even the greatest tragedy, the bitterest persecution, the worst misfortune, or death of the body can do any permanent harm or separate us from the love of God!* (see Rom. 8:35).

This confidence in the faithfulness of God is available only through God's enabling grace. Reflecting on this empowering and sustaining grace reminded the administrator of a profound experience that occurred during the summer of 2002.

He and his wife celebrated their 40th wedding anniversary in June

2002 on a summer weekend in New York City. Each day they were in the Big Apple, they walked around Ground Zero. They were *overwhelmed* by the huge number of pictures, cards, tributes, letters, and prayers attached to anything and everything around the perimeter, and they paused and read many of them.

In the midst of such grief and tragedy, the administrator found himself singing over and over again the chorus of the old hymn "The Solid Rock":

> *On Christ, the solid Rock, I stand;*
> *All other ground is sinking sand.*
> *All other ground is sinking sand.*

Verse two of the song, written in 1834 by Edward Mote, seemed especially appropriate on this occasion in 2002:

> *When darkness seems to hide His face,*
> *I rest on His unchanging grace.*
> *In every high and stormy gale,*
> *My anchor holds within the veil.*[1]

Christians and servant leaders place their hope in Christ! By grace alone, they affirm this hope among those suffering from economic deprivation, vast social disparity, political dictatorships, or the hideous work of terrorists.

Their hope as Christians is in the God of Abraham, Isaac, and Jacob, the God who was in Christ reconciling the world unto himself. *The center of the Christian gospel is the reconciliation of all creation to God through Jesus Christ.* The title of the old gospel song has it right, "This World Is Not My Home." Christians are to live in the world but not be of the world.

For Christian leaders, their hope is not for this life only but for life eternal with the triune God. The question they face as followers of Jesus Christ is this: Are they living faithfully as members of the "community of the King," with Kingdom "eyes," ruthless trust, and a radical hope?

The administrator and his family lived in Manila, the Philippines, prior to moving in 1989 to Mount Vernon. At the time, the average per capita income was $700 a year. They worshipped with beautiful Filipino Christians whose joy was contagious. Their church facilities were simple. Their homes were modest. Many traveled to the market each day for food because there was no refrigeration in their homes.

Yet, these Christians were joyful because their hope was not in their government, their job, or their income. Their hope was in Jesus Christ for their *salvation* and for *their comfort*. They truly believed that "this world is not my home."

Hope in Christ does not mean for servant leaders that they will avoid or be able to ignore suffering. They know that hope born of faith is nurtured and purified through pain, suffering, and difficulty. The basis of their hope, however, has to do with the One who is stronger than the suffering they encounter.

The people of Israel repeatedly reflected on their history and discerned God's guiding hand in the many painful events. *Memory reminds the people of God of the faithfulness of God in the hard times and in the joyful moments.* Without memory, there is no expectation.

With expectation, they experience the minutes, hours, and days of life differently. Christian hope is not dependent on peace in the land or justice in the world. Hope is willing to leave some questions unanswered. Hope makes you see God's guiding hand not only in the gentle and pleasant moments but also in the shadows of disappointment and darkness. Why? Because servant leaders believe! And because they believe, servant leaders offer their lives to Christ as a living sacrifice.

May grace, peace, and hope come to servant leaders as they reflect upon the leadership "hope" of reconciliation and transformation—individually and collectively—especially in difficult and confusing times!

Leaders are dealers in hope. Servant leaders radiate Christian hope in confusing and conflicting times in a community of faith. Amen!

NOTES

Introduction

1. J. Kenneth Grider and Thomas C. Oden, *A Wesleyan-Holiness Theology* (Kansas City: Beacon Hill Press of Kansas City, 1994), 526-27.

Chapter 1

1. E. Dee Freeborn, Janine Tartaglia, Wesley Tracy, and Morris Weigelt, *The Upward Call: Spiritual Formation and the Holy Life* (Kansas City: Beacon Hill Press of Kansas City, 1994), 18.

2. Dietrich Bonhoeffer, *Life Together: The Classic Exploration of Faith in Community* (San Francisco: Harper & Row, 1978), 104.

3. Elton Trueblood, *Your Other Vocation* (New York: Harper & Brothers, 1952), 161.

Chapter 3

1. Henri J. M. Nouwen, *In the Name of Jesus: Reflections on Christian Leadership* (New York: Crossroad, 1995), 69.

2. Ibid., 13, 33, 53.

3. Ibid., 22.

4. Ibid., 50.

5. Ibid., 60.

6. Ibid., 68.

7. Ibid., 72.

8. Virginia Satir, *Peoplemaking* (Palo Alto, Calif.: Science and Behavior Books, 1972), 30.

Chapter 4

1. John Powell, *Why Am I Afraid to Tell You Who I Am?* (Allen, Tex.: Thomas More Publishing, reprint edition, 1995).

2. David W. Augsburger, *Caring Enough to Confront* (Ventura, Calif.: Regal Books, 1981), 53.

3. Satir, *Peoplemaking*, 78.

Chapter 5

1. Bonhoeffer, *Life Together,* 92.

2. Henri Nouwen, *The Way of the Heart: Desert Spirituality and Contemporary Ministry* (San Francisco: Harper San Francisco, reprint edition, 1991), 47.

3. Ibid., 48.

4. Ibid., 51.

Chapter 6

1. Theodore Roosevelt, address at the Sorbonne, Paris, April 23, 1910, Bartleby.com, http://www.bartleby.com/73/10.html (accessed March 12, 2008).

2. Jim Collins, *Good to Great: Why Some Companies Make the Leap . . . and Others Don't* (New York: HarperCollins Publishers Inc., 2001), 198.

Chapter 8

1. Robert K. Greenleaf, *Servant Leadership: A Journey into the Nature of Legitimate Power and Greatness* (New York: Paulist Press, 2002), 96.
2. Ibid.
3. Source unknown.
4. John C. Maxwell and Jim Dornan, *Becoming a Person of Influence* (Nashville: Thomas Nelson, 1997), 40.

Chapter 9

1. John C. Bowling, *Grace-Full Leadership* (Kansas City: Beacon Hill Press of Kansas City, 2000), 11, 75.
2. Trueblood, *Your Other Vocation*, 32.

Chapter 10

1. Greenleaf, *Servant Leadership*, 6.
2. James M. Kouzes and Barry Z. Posner, *The Leadership Challenge* (San Francisco: John Wiley and Sons, Inc., 2002), 305.
3. Jackson W. Carroll, *Mainline to the Future* (Louisville, Ky.: Westminster John Knox Press, 2000), 8.

Chapter 11

1. John Wesley, "A Covenant Prayer," adapted in *Sing to the Lord* (Kansas City: Lillenas Publishing Co., 1993), 484.
2. Alan E. Nelson, *Broken in the Right Place: How God Tames the Soul* (Nashville: Thomas Nelson, 1994), 7.

Chapter 12

1. Brennan Manning, presented at a chapel meeting attended by one of the authors and held at Mount Vernon Nazarene University.
2. Ibid.

Chapter 13

1. Brennan Manning, *Ruthless Trust: The Ragamuffin's Path to God* (New York: HarperCollins Publishers Inc., 2000), 133-35.
2. Idries Shah, *The Way of the Sufi* (New York: E.P. Dutton & Co., Inc., 1970), 207ff., quoted by Sheldon B. Kopp, *If You Meet the Buddha on the Road, Kill Him!* (Palo Alto, Calif.: Science and Behavior Books, Inc., 1972), 8.

Chapter 14

1. Henri Nouwen, Donald P. McNeil, and Douglas A. Morrison, *Compassion: A Reflection on Christian Life* (New York: Image Books, reprint edition, 1983), 63.

Chapter 15

1. Letter to one of the authors from a former student.
2. Anne and Ray Ortlund, *Mastering Ministry* (Carol Stream, Ill.: Multnomah Press, 1992), 92.

3. For complete story see Alfred Lansing, *Endurance: Shackleton's Incredible Voyage* (New York: Carroll and Graf Publishers, 1998).

4. Dennis N. T. Perkins, Margaret P. Holtman, and Paul R. Kessler, *Leading at the Edge: Leadership Lessons from the Extraordinary Expedition of Shackleton's Antarctic Expedition* (New York: Amacom: American Management Association, 2000), 88.

5. Stan Toler and Jerry Brecheisen, *Lead to Succeed: New Testament Principles for Visionary Leadership* (Kansas City: Beacon Hill Press of Kansas City, 2003), 116.

Postscript
1. Ken Bible, ed., *Sing to the Lord* (Kansas City: Lillenas Publishing Company, 1993), 436.